THE ISLANDS SERIES

SINGAPORE

THE ISLANDS SERIES

* Published in the United States by Stackpole
† Published in the United States by David & Charles

SINGAPORE

by SALLY BACKHOUSE

DAVID & CHARLES : NEWTON ABBOT

STACKPOLE BOOKS : HARRISBURG

This edition first published in 1972
in Great Britain by
David & Charles (Publishers) Limited Newton Abbot Devon
in the United States in 1973 by
Stackpole Books Harrisburg Pa

ISBN 0 7153 5683 6   (*Great Britain*)

ISBN 0 8117 1541 8 (*United States*)

To Barbara Drew

*Set in eleven on thirteen point Baskerville
and printed in Great Britain by
Clarke Doble & Brendon Limited Plymouth*

CONTENTS

ILLUSTRATIONS

ILLUSTRATIONS

A note on place names in Singapore:

A few parts of Singapore have undergone one or more changes of name over the years and this sometimes leads to confusion. The name appropriate to the period under discussion is used in the text, since the original names are met with in many of the books mentioned in the bibliography. The varieties of nomenclature are given below, in chronological order.

British Naval Base = Sembawang shipyard.
Bukit Larangan (Forbidden Hill) = Government Hill = Fort Canning.
Commercial Square = Raffles Place.
New Harbour = Keppel Harbour.
Pulau Blakang Mati = Sentosa.

The term 'Esplanade' and its Malay equivalent, *Padang*, have been used concurrently over the years to denote the open ground fronting the present Supreme Court Building.

7

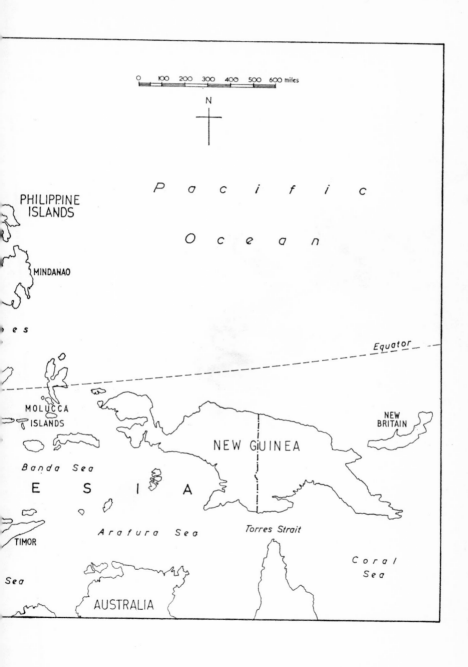

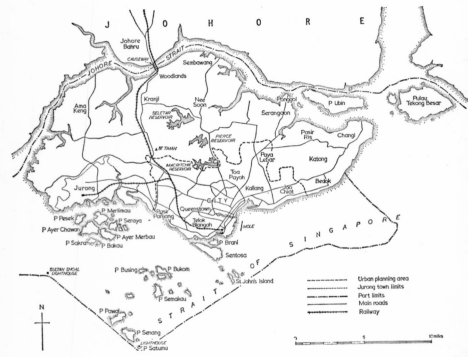

THE REPUBLIC OF SINGAPORE

1 INTRODUCTION

For Singapore, position is all. This tiny island city-state, which would fit more than five times over into Rhode Island and has a population less than that of West Berlin, has assumed many roles in its history, but in all of them its location has been of prime importance. It lies just off the tip of the Malay Peninsula, a long tongue of land which stretches south from Thailand into the area bounded by Sumatra on the west, the other Indonesian islands on the south, and Borneo to the east. Singapore thus commands an entrance to the Indian Ocean, the South China Sea, and the Java Sea alike. Barely 1° N of the equator, it has been, since the first days of commercial flights, a staging point between north and south as well as between east and west. In terms of flying miles it is almost equidistant between Zurich and Honolulu and between Perth and New Delhi.

In ancient times it became an outpost of the Javanese empire of Majapahit, and later a focus of its rivalry with Siam; it was known to Indian, Chinese and Arab traders long before the Christian conquerors arrived. Re-founded as a British trading settlement little more than 150 years ago, Singapore turned from an almost desert island into an *entrepôt* which drew to itself like a magnet the rich and varied produce of the countries lying around it. Today it is the world's fourth busiest port.

Anomalies abound in the history of Singapore. Geographically and economically part of the Malay world, surrounded by Malay-speaking peoples and ruled by Europeans, it became a predominantly Chinese city, though with substantial minorities of Malays

11

and Indians. Between 1942 and 1945 it was an arena where the scores of earlier Sino-Japanese conflict were settled, and to the world at large it was notorious as the 'impregnable fortress' which collapsed like a house of cards and brought down with it the myth of British invulnerability in the East.

The postwar struggle for independence, common to many parts of the world at this period, in Singapore revealed unique features. The People's Action Party government, which has had an all-important influence on Singapore's recent development, was led by Lee Kuan Yew, who rode to power on the back of the communist tiger. He not only survived against all the odds, but set up a form of 'guided democracy' which treads a fine line between popular government as the West knows it and authoritarian rule in the traditions of old China.

At the traveller's first glance, Singapore seems to wear its Asian character lightly : the waterfront and central business area are thick with skyscrapers; the streets, empty of beggars, are full of modern cars and people wearing Western clothes; and the standard of cleanliness is high. Yet four distinct civilisations have gone to make the republic what it is, and one has only to linger a while in one of the oldest thoroughfares, such as Hill Street, to be aware of it. If one stands in the tiny green graveyard of the Armenian Church there, amid the broken stones commemorating such pioneer figures as Catchick Moses, Fort Canning, once the Forbidden Hill of ancient Malay peoples, is directly behind. To the right, the ornate façade of the Masonic Hall recalls the days of the British colony; on the left, the modern elegance of the American Embassy suggests Singapore's growing world importance. Directly facing the churchyard is St Gregory's Place, with its two-storey shophouses in traditional style and glimpses of the flowerpots and balconies of rooftop apartments. There, Chinese tailors, cobblers and coffee-shop owners ply their trade in shops open to the street; and along the five-foot way the open-air barber sets chairs for his customers. Trishaw drivers cycle past, pedalling their passengers along with painful effort; the smell of

12

curry from a famous Indian restaurant drifts down the street. Walk a little further along from the Armenian Church, towards Stamford Road and over the ground that was once a spice grove belonging to the East India Company, and you will pass the flamboyant Chinese Chamber of Commerce and the tiny Burhani mosque squeezed in next to it. Across the road, Portugal, China and India have left their separate legacies on the shop signs : the D'Cotta Clinic is neighbour to the Chong Nam Press and the local branch of the Red Swastika Society. The shop of the Chinese medicine man stands next to the modern drug store, where, at lunchtime, the assistants eat their meal at the counter using chopsticks. This is the Singapore of many races and of much change swiftly accomplished.

The smallest and most densely populated state in South East Asia, Singapore is one of the 'developing countries' of the world which yet has little in common with the others in the East. In contrast to them, its population is essentially urban rather than agricultural; industrialisation is already well advanced and is proceeding rapidly; with a standard of living second in Asia only to that of Japan, most of its population is well-fed, well-housed and reasonably well-educated.

Yet all has been achieved in the face of many difficulties and some dangerous failures, including that of the brief period of union with Malaysia. Singapore's size and position at once favour it and put it at risk. Easy to administer, the island is short of living space. The position which makes it a great *entrepôt* makes it also peculiarly sensitive to recessions in world trade and to outside political pressures. Because of its multi-racial population, adhering to a medley of religions, languages and customs, it is not certain that it can be moulded into a nation, not of Chinese, Malays or Indians, but of Singaporeans. Yet this is the policy which its government has been pursuing over the last decade or so, pressing the separate races not only towards mutual tolerance but towards becoming bi- or tri-lingual, with English as their passport to modernisation. As Lee Kuan Yew himself said in a speech in 1966 : 'This community has no built-in reflexes : loyalty, patriotism, history, tradition . . . your population still cannot identify the future of the individual with the future of the community . . . which means a re-orientation, a re-shuffling of emphasis of our various inherited values'. Singapore has come a long way since those words were spoken, but the degree of the re-shuffling, and the nature of the values which will finally emerge give it a very special interest to observers of world history and of the political and social relations between people of different races.

2   PHYSICAL ENVIRONMENT

THE republic of Singapore comprises the island of Singapore itself, plus some fifty-four small islands within its territorial waters. Roughly eighty-five miles north of the equator, it is situated between 1° 09′ N and 1° 29′ N latitude and 103° 38′ E and 104° 06′ E longitude, and is almost in the centre of the Sundaland region, an area which includes the Malay Peninsula, Borneo, and Java and Sumatra and their adjacent small islands. These territories are surrounded by a zone of shallow sea, all of which is less than 100 fathoms and most of which is less than fifty fathoms deep. The fauna of the Sundaland area is uniform, and the region is one of the richest in the world for the variety of plant and animal life. The island of Singapore, separated from the Malay Peninsula by the Straits of Johore, measures approximately twenty-six miles from east to west and fourteen miles from north to south, and has an area of about 209·5 square miles, at present being added to by reclamation. Including the small islands, the total area is 225·6 square miles.

GEOLOGY

The geology of Singapore displays three groups of rocks, each occurring in well defined areas, and each being covered by recent deposits. The oldest group, in the west and south, are the sedimentary rocks, complexly folded and faulted. The layers of clay and sand overlying the older schist may date back to Upper Palaeozoic times. In the north central areas, igneous rocks, possibly of Mesozoic or Tertiary age, have intruded the sedimentary rocks, forming a granite batholith with a number of pegmatite veins and dolorite and porphyry dykes. To the north-east, at Changi, another intrusion occurs in which the main rock is a metamorphosed hornblende soda granite cut by lamporphyric dykes. In general, however, the east is covered by Older Alluvium, the occurrence of which is related to changing sealevels during the Pleistocene period. Some geologists believe it represents the older terraces of the Johore river. The recent deposits include poorly consolidated gravels, sands, clays, mud and pebble beds, and corals along the coast. There is no limestone or other calcareous rock on the island. The poor quality of the soil has helped to throw extra emphasis on Singapore's role as an *entrepôt* port and, latterly, an industrial centre : agriculturally it has never been very productive.

RELIEF AND DRAINAGE

The relief of the western and southern parts of Singapore island is dominated by ridges trending from north-west to south-east. The central granite plateau has been reduced by erosion and weathering, especially rapid because of the high temperatures and abundant rainfall, to high rounded hills and spurs. Steep hills along the western boundary of the batholith include Bukit Timah, at 581ft the highest ground on the island, Bukit Gombak (437ft), Bukit Panjang (434ft), and Bukit Mandai (422ft), but many of the lower hills of the island have been levelled in the course of reclamation. Almost 64 per cent of the land is less than 50ft above sealevel, and only 10 per cent is more than 100ft. Ten per cent of the island's area consists of plains, which are mainly to be found on the south coast, the two largest being at the combined Kallang-Geylang estuaries in the east, and at Jurong in the west. Singapore has no significant mineral deposits. Clay is extracted in small quantities, the land affected being less than 100 acres to the west of the island. In the same area, and somewhat to the north, granite quarries, mostly established in the postwar period, operate over about 250 acres, of which not more than half is actually quarried. Sand-washing, which began to flourish during the late 1950s and continued under the influence of the housing boom, has now been brought under public control by the issue of licences, but has eroded and laid waste small eastern areas round Tampines and Ulu Bedok.

The pattern of drainage is extremely complex, owing to the heavy rainfall and the varied nature of the terrain, and many of the rivers are scarcely more than streams : the longest is the Sungei Seletar, about nine miles in all. There are more than forty drainage basins, of which thirty are less than five square miles each in area. The central catchment area of about $12\frac{3}{4}$ square miles has three reservoirs and many small streams.

CLIMATE

The climate of Singapore is essentially equatorial, but equable, owing to the modifying influence of the sea. The average daytime maximum temperature is 87° F (30·6° C), which drops to an average minimum of 75° F (24° C) at night. The temperature rarely falls below 70° F or rises above 94° F. Although there is no distinct wet or dry season, rainfall tends to be heaviest during the first half of the north-east monsoon, from November to January. The south-west monsoon blows from June to September, and July is usually the driest and sunniest month, though *Sumatras*, violent squalls of wind and rain caused by the obstruction offered to the monsoon by the mountains of Sumatra, are characteristic from May to October. Thunderstorms, though often violent, seldom last more than an hour.

The earth tremors felt in Singapore five or six times during the nineteenth century have all been attributed to the activity of volcanoes elsewhere in the region. During the spectacular eruption of Krakatoa, in August 1883, a loud explosion interrupted the chanting of the psalms at evensong in St Andrew's Cathedral. Further rumblings were heard during the night, and a day or

B

two later pieces of pumice stone 'as big as a hat' were found floating outside the harbour. There have been no similar occurrences in the twentieth century, and Singapore is untroubled by the typhoons, cyclones or earthquakes which ravage other parts of Asia.

Without the benefits of air-conditioning, which is widely available in hotels and public buildings, the modern traveller is likely to be made uncomfortable not by the heat so much as by the relative humidity, which is often above 95 per cent just before sunrise, and about 65 per cent on dry afternoons. Rudyard Kipling found it like being in an orchid house—'a clinging, remorseless, steam-sweat that knows no variation between night and day'—but most would agree that its discomfort is mitigated by the sea breezes which reach a considerable part of the island.

	J	F	M	A	M	J	Jy	A	S	O	N	D	Annual
A	78	79	80	81	81	81	81	81	81	80	79	78	80
B	85	83	84	85	84	83	82	83	83	84	86	86	84
C	10·0	7·0	7·7	7·4	6·8	6·8	6·4	7·3	6·7	8·0	10·0	10·9	95

A   Mean 24-hour temperature F°
B   Relative humidity per cent 24-hour mean
C   Average monthly rainfall in inches

The weather : based on thirty-two years of Meteorological Department records.

FLORA

Despite the destruction over the last 150 years of much of the original vegetation, more than 2,000 species of higher plants and about 155 species of ferns are still to be found in Singapore. Plant life has been determined by the low relief and the equatorial climate, and it is essentially akin to, though in some respects poorer than, that of the Malay Peninsula. In 1819, at the time of the British settlement, the island was almost entirely covered by thick vegetation. Nearly two-thirds of Singapore supported

18

primary rain forest, interrupted by a few clearings made by Chinese cultivators. The coastal area consisted largely of mangrove swamp, which was also extensive on the right bank of the Singapore river. These coastal swamps were presumably exposed when the sealevel retreated during the Pleistocene period. Freshwater swamp forest had developed in a few lowland areas of the interior which were periodically waterlogged and became flooded. Between Changi Point and Tanjong Rhu a coastal belt of casuarina and low scrub known as *belukar* grew in areas too small to support the forest.

After 1819, the destruction of vegetation was rapid and widespread, as the forest was cleared for nutmeg and pepper plantations, and used as fuel in the preparation of gambier. By 1859, 45,000 acres lay waste and overrun by *belukar,* having been abandoned after cultivation. In 1884, forest reserves totalling 8,000 acres were established. Even then, people were allowed to cut timber for firewood, except on Bukit Timah, so the primary forest, virtually impossible to replace once it is destroyed, gradually gave way to secondary forest. Today, only two areas of primary rain forest remain : one of 163 acres in the Bukit Timah reserve, and an 11 acre plot in the Botanic Gardens. Singapore is, with Rio de Janeiro, the only major city with a tropical forest reserve in its centre.

The primary forest is characterised by a very wide variety of trees, which form a canopy over sixty feet above the ground. These are interspersed with much taller shorea trees (the average height is 150–80ft) and sometimes by short shade-loving trees. The primary forest includes wild species of the durian, breadfruit, mangosteen, rambutan, nutmeg and mango, and oaks with evergreen leaves. Many of its trees bear fruits, flowers and leaves at heights inaccessible to the botanist, and before World War II *berok* monkeys were specially trained to bring down such plants in the Botanic Gardens.

Secondary forest is more difficult to penetrate, since it occurs on riverbanks and in clearings where sunlight reaches the ground, and its trees are thickly surrounded by various shrubs and climbers. It provides an abundance of algae, mosses and liverworts, lichens, orchids and ferns. Its trees, less tall than those of the primary forest, are more closely set : they include the pompom, the *tiup-tiup* and the silverback.

The saltwater mangrove swamps, which are subject to tidal inundations, were until recent years the most extensive remaining forests, but are now disappearing as a result of reclamation schemes carried out by the government. Much ground has been recently drained in the Jurong Pandan area on the west coast, and in the Seletar-Tampines area of the north-east. Kranji nature reserve, on the north coast, is the last remaining area of mangrove forest officially protected, but other extensive areas still exist in the west. Along the coast there is a wide variety of marine habitats, ranging from mangrove swamps and mudflats to rocky shores and coral reefs. Near Nee Soon, areas of freshwater swamp remain, perpetuated by periodic flooding and supporting small trees such as the leechwood in their acid peaty depths. There is a small area of hot springs near the village of Umum, on the island of Tekong Besar.

In addition to the forested and swamp areas, much of Singapore is still covered by *belukar*, or by *lalang*, a tall coarse grass, both of which occur on areas abandoned after cultivation and are difficult to get rid of. *Belukar* is extensive on Mount Faber, in the Ulu Pandan, Ayer Rajah and Clementi Road areas, and on several of the offshore islands.

In an island which, despite the areas of scrub, is green with an equatorial luxuriance, the flora of Singapore provides its greatest beauty. Wayside flowers—some of them, such as the blue giant Thunbergia and the yellow blackeyed susan, having been introduced from other tropical countries—blossom all the year round. They include the yellow trimezia, the holly rose, the *pulut-pulut*, the twelve o'clock flower, the snake's tongue and the yellow wood sorrel. Also to be seen are the shrew bean, the elephant's foot, vernonia, the star of bethlehem, the heliotrope and various members of the figwort family. On open wasteground the Singapore rhododendron is common. Orchids, described by John Cameron in 1865 as ubiquitous and without value, are now most easily seen under commercial cultivation, but some, like the pigeon orchid, a tree dweller, are still found wild. Outstanding amongst the plants of the forest are the insectivorous pitcher plants or 'monkey cups'. Among the freshwater plants, algae of several colours are prominent; also various kinds of ferns and the water hyacinth, and there are several submerged plants, including the Malayan eel grass and the hydrilla.

Singapore has many spectacular flowering trees, such as the golden angsana, various species of eugenia, including the clove and jambu, the albizzia, and trees introduced from abroad such as the red flame tree, several species of cassia, and the African tulip tree. Most fragrant of the flowering trees is the plumeria or frangipani, also known as the temple tree, which blooms in various colours in the Botanic Gardens.

Cameron also wrote that the whole island breathed 'lovely forest perfumes' at night, and this is still true of Singapore's many gardens. The first idea of making Singapore a 'garden city' was mooted in 1957. Since then the parks and trees division of the Public Works Department has planted thousands of trees and flowering shrubs, so that Singapore is now perhaps the greenest city in Asia.

Rhu and coconut trees grow along the seashores, and have also been planted inland. Cultivated fruit trees include the mango, which was introduced from India, the soursop, custard apple, guava and papaya, and the durian, so delicious in flavour, so repulsive in smell, and said to have been described by a disapproving Scotswoman as 'a maist unchaste fruit'.

The Botanic Gardens were established on their present site in 1859, when the government gave a grant of 50 acres for the purpose to a newly formed private organisation, the Singapore Agri-horticultural Society, and they were opened to the public in 1874. In the 1820s, Sir Thomas Stamford Raffles, founder of

21

modern Singapore, had supported the idea of establishing such gardens, and the first ground used for the purpose had been laid out on the slopes of Fort Canning across what is now the Stamford Canal, as far as Bras Basah Road. The present Botanic Gardens has one of the finest collections of palms in the world, and an orchid collection of about 500 species. The hybridisation of orchids has been pursued at the gardens since 1928, and many internationally known hybrids have been produced. The Singapore Herbarium, established in 1880, has a dried-plant collection of nearly 500,000 specimens of the known flora of the Malay Peninsula.

FAUNA

Singapore, in spite of its small size, has more species of mammal than Great Britain, though they have been greatly reduced by human depredation. They are mainly the same as in the Malay Peninsula, but the large wild mammals are notably absent : no tiger has been seen wild since 1932, although it is known they used to swim across from the Straits of Johore. Throughout the nineteenth century they were a serious menace to human life, lurking along the edges of newly cut roads and, as late as 1865, killing a man a day on average.

Leopards are now extinct in Singapore, though the leopard cat is still to be found. Mousedeer abound in the catchment area forest, in which the flying lemur, the flying squirrel, and the porcupine are also seen. Squirrels and tree shrews live in the Botanic Gardens, where the long-tailed macaque monkey, found in several other parts of the island, runs wild. The pangolin or scaly anteater lives in the region of Nee Soon. The musang, a large cat-like arboreal creature, may be found on the roofs of houses even in the central area, where bats are still common and the house shrew scuttles along the monsoon drain. Native species of rat exist in *belukar* and in the forest, but the larger Norway rat and the little house rat are introduced pests.

By tropical standards the variety of birds is rather disappointing, though many locally resident or from other countries may be studied at close quarters in the Jurong Bird Park, opened in 1970. The amateur birdwatcher finds much to interest him in Singapore suburban gardens, where the yellow-vented bulbul, the mina, and the pied triller may be seen, and sometimes the white-collared kingfisher. The tree sparrow (the same species as in Europe), the Malay house swift, some kinds of swallow, and the Java sparrow are still to be found in the town, along with crows, which also haunt the seashore, and there are doves in the suburbs. The black-naped oriole, a seasonal visitor, provides a dramatic flash of colour, like the white cattle egrets that come in winter to the rural areas. Scrubland birds include the coucals and brainfever birds, and quails and pipits are to be found in grassland. Barbets, jewel thrushes and malcohas inhabit the forest; birds of prey include the changeable hawk eagle and the white-tailed sea eagle, which is often seen inland; and the weaver finch, which nests in colonies with bottleshaped hanging nests, still has its haunts at Pasir Panjang and in one or two other places. Interesting marine birds are the brahminy kite and the tern, both common. For a more comprehensive list, including winter visitors, the reader may consult D. S. Johnson's *Introduction to the Natural History of Singapore*.

Most mammals and birds are protected in Singapore, and no collecting of plants or animals is allowed in the nature reserves without special permission.

Everyone who lives in Singapore must be aware of the *chichak*, the tiny house lizard which is often seen walking upside down on the ceiling. The beautiful green tree lizard and the flying lizard frequent suburban gardens and tree-clad areas. Skinks are found on the grass and in drains, and there are water monitors which sometimes grow to over four feet in length. The estuarine crocodile has virtually disappeared as a result of land development, though very occasionally one is seen in the north-west.

Most indigenous snakes are non-poisonous, and less common than in other tropical areas. They include the house snake, the striped kukri snake and the paradise tree snake. The grassgreen whip snake lives only in trees. Pythons up to twenty-five feet in length may be seen, and a dangerous snake sometimes found in residential areas is the spitting cobra. King cobras, though uncommon, are occasionally found round the catchments. Very few cases of snake bite have been recorded, though the banded krait, the coral snake and the pit viper, which live in the trees of mangrove swamps, also occur. Toads are ubiquitous. The crab-eating frog is itself often eaten as a delicacy. Singapore also boasts one of the world's largest frogs, the Malayan giant frog, which may grow to ten inches in length. After heavy rain the loud call of the Malayan bull frog is heard by the wayside. Other noisy creatures are grasshoppers and crickets. House pests include cockroaches and termites.

Scorpions are found, as are giant centipedes, mainly in the forest, though they are not uncommon in the suburbs. There are many species of spider, including the hairy huntsman, which eats cockroaches, and jumping and fishing spiders. Often seen in houses are the carpenter bee, which nests in timber, and the potter wasp, which may build on interior walls the urn-shaped pot where it lays its eggs. Occasionally, in scrubland, dangerous hornets hang their nests from trees or bushes. There are many thousand kinds of beetle in Singapore, and fireflies are abundant in the mangrove swamps. Cameron tells how the Malays used to imprison them as living jewels in 'little round cages about the size of a pea', worn in place of precious stones for part of the night and then set free.

Houseflies do not flourish to any extent, and government measures have considerably reduced the incidence of mosquitoes. The plague-carrying oriental rat flea is known, but the disease is not. Ants and snails exist in large numbers, the commonest land snail having been introduced from Africa. Butterflies and moths are very well represented, the largest moth being the atlas.

Freshwater creatures include water snakes, the black pond

tortoise and, in the catchment area, the Malayan mud turtle. There are between twenty and forty species of freshwater fish, almost all of them in the Seletar Basin. The most common fish in the forest streams is the Malayan barb. The golden Singapore minnow is peculiar to Singapore in ponds and open streams around the catchment area. Unusual species include the catfish, the *ikan keli*, found everywhere outside the forest; it is an air-breather which can cross short stretches of dry land. The swamp eel, also an air-breather, can survive for long periods buried in the ground. The largest freshwater prawn, the *udang galah*, may grow to over ten inches in length. Freshwater sponges occasionally occur.

Marine life is diverse and fascinating and shows special forms in saline or brackish water where streams run into the sea. The water of the seas round Singapore is always less saline than that of the neighbouring open seas because of the large amounts of freshwater discharged by the rivers of Singapore and of Johore. Salinity seldom exceeds 32 per cent. There are at least 150 species of marine prawns. 'Living fossils' occur, such as the lingula, which seems to have come down without fundamental change from Palaeozoic times. The king crabs are almost equally old. Although sharks and barracudas are quite common, they seldom attack man, who has more to fear from the venomous catfish *ikan sembilang*, the stone fish, the cone shells, and such jellyfish as the fire medusa. Dolphins appear off the Raffles Lighthouse, particularly during the north-east monsoon. The green turtle is quite common.

Openwater fish include flying fish and pomfrets and, in the shallow offshore waters, shoals of small fish such as tamban, anchovies, scads and croakers are to be found. Spanish mackerel are common and large fish include the dorab, which makes nearly vertical leaps. Some fish dwell in the mud on the seabed, including flatheads, gobies and the stargazers, which have eyes on top of their heads. The sting-ray is common, but the electric ray is rarer. Prawns, lobsters and hermit crabs are to be found everywhere. The phosphorescent waves seen at night are usually caused by noctiluca, a luminous flagellate occurring in sea plankton.

The mangrove swamps, inundated with seawater twice daily and served with freshwater by rain and streams, display special forms amongst their teeming animal life. Common in such a habitat are oysters, barnacles, snails, and the mudlobsters, which make mud chimneys. The crabs include the fiddler crab, which signals to attract females with one greatly enlarged and brightly coloured claw. The range of animal life is diversified by the herons, the kingfishers, the pythons and geckoes which live in the trees of the mangrove swamp.

Yet another type of habitat is provided by the reefs, about thirty miles of which are close to the main land mass or islands. Here live sea cucumbers, sea urchins, starfish, giant clams, sea anemones, and the egg-laying seasnake, which is highly venomous but has never been known to attack man. Beautiful fishes, such as the coral-eating pirate fish, abound on the reef slope. Eighty-four species of coral have been recorded.

Silt and oil pollution in Singapore's offshore waters threaten to destroy some of the marine life formerly found there, and in common with the depredation of commercial collectors, have interfered with the growth of coral formations. But in 1971 an act of parliament made it an offence punishable by heavy fine to pollute Singapore waters, and special measures are taken to clear up oil slicks quickly. Meanwhile, coral culture experiments are being carried out by the University of Singapore Fisheries Biology Unit and the Regional Marine Biological Centre. The Van Kleef Aquarium, opened in 1955, has a relatively small but interesting collection of marine and freshwater fish.

URBAN DEVELOPMENT

History

Far reaching changes caused by the urban renewal programme and the dispersal of population to satellite towns are altering the face of Singapore in the 1970s. The transformation is taking place to a degree and with a rapidity probably unparalleled elsewhere in the world. The business centre is being torn down and rebuilt piece by piece, and the forms of land use throughout the island are being extensively reorganised. The reasons for change are both economic and political. In previous decades, however, the distribution of population and the layout of the city continued largely on the lines of the original plan laid down by Sir Thomas Stamford Raffles.

	Percentage
Agricultural Land . . . . ₂	24·5
Water Catchment and Forest Reserves ₃ . . .	6·0
British Military and Naval Bases . ₃ . .	10·5
City, Jurong and other Built-up Areas . . ₃ .	35·0
Swamps and Water Areas	9·5
Vacant and Underdeveloped Land . ₇ . . ₃	14·5

LAND USE

Based on the 1967 Land and Building Use Survey (surrounding small islands excluded)

When Raffles landed in 1819, to start a British trading settlement, the island was almost entirely covered by jungle, the area south of the Singapore river was swampland, and in the early years up to 1,000 labourers daily worked at clearing the jungle and erecting buildings.

Attracted by the safe anchorage and the possibility of sinking wells and of building, Raffles provided for the spacious area reserved for government purposes on the left bank of the Singapore river which remains in essentials today. Men of many nationalities flocked to the new trading centre, and the various main communities were each allotted their place. The Arabs and Bugis were allowed to live in an area between the coast, the Rochore river, and the outlying swamp, clustering round the residence of the Temenggong, the leader of the small band of Malays who lived on the island before Raffles' arrival. The oldest part of the town proper is this grid of parallel streets from Beach Road inland as far as Bencoolen Street. The Chinese were allotted a settlement on the right bank of the river forming the nucleus of Chinatown, which remained until recently the most densely populated part of Singapore. The earliest Indian traders settled along the western edge of the central business area, round what became Chulia Street, Market Street, and High Street, where many are still to be found. The Malays and *orang laut*, the aboriginals who lived in boats or in houses built on stilts over the water, for the most part continued to live by fishing on the coast.

With the use of the soil from a nearby hill, the mudflat which became Commercial Square was filled in under the direction of the town planning committee set up by Raffles. The first Indian convict labour arrived in 1825, and both banks of the river in the central area had been cleared of vegetation and fully developed by 1830. The administrative centre remained on the east, whilst the western side of the settlement was devoted largely to commerce and trade. Consequently Boat Quay on the Singapore river became the very heart of Singapore, and so remained until the end of the nineteenth century. The Elgin bridge was the first to join the opposite banks of the river: a wooden structure built in 1823 joined the present North and South Bridge Roads, and an iron bridge was built there in 1862, at which time it received its current name. In 1840 Coleman's brick bridge connected Hill Street with New Bridge Road.

The peculiar circumstances of Singapore's commercial development encouraged an intense concentration of population in the area of Raffles' original settlement. Since Singapore's wealth, for over a century, came almost entirely from its *entrepôt* trade, activity remained centred close to the port and the Singapore river. The situation was confirmed by the opening up of the P & O Company at New Harbour, and the subsequent development of the Tanjong Pagar Dock Company and its virtual monopoly from the 1860s onward. The tradition among the Chinese and Indians of residing at their place of work intensified the trend.

Raffles had made plans, issued in November 1822, for a grid

pattern of streets with the main roads running parallel to the harbour and the secondary roads crossing them at right angles, and this pattern remains. In Chinatown, shophouses were built from about 1842 onwards. Originally these were single-storey buildings with a 12–16ft frontage and a depth of from 100 to 200 feet. They comprised one room open to the street for business, and another room at the back where workmen and the family lived. As immigrants arrived in ever increasing numbers, one or two upper storeys were added. Later these were divided and sub-divided into cubicles, so that in recent times scores of people might live in such a house. These shophouses, with their character-istic verandah roofs supported by pillars and sheltering the 'five-foot way', gave old Singapore much of its architectural character. Shophouses built in the early twentieth century still stand, often decorated with patterns of acanthus leaves and mock Corinthian pillars, and colour-washed in brilliant pinks, blues and greens.

The richest Chinese merchants moved into the houses of the central area when, beginning in the 1840s, these were deserted by the European merchants for the fringes of River Valley Road and Orchard Road. The pattern of living set by these Europeans, in bungalows separated from each other by large leafy gardens, persists today, though there are now many semi-detached and terrace houses, and the suburbs promise to encircle the island. A few houses of the beautiful early style, imitating features seen in Malay dwellings, still exist in places such as Tanglin and the Cluny Road area. Raised from the ground on stilts, high-ceilinged and with an open verandah running the width of the house, they are both cool and gracious. One of the oldest scheduled for preservation is 'Bellevue', built by Dr Thomas Oxley in 1842.

As the island jungle was gradually cleared, the settlement spread out west of Chinatown along Havelock Road and Tiong Bahru, eastward towards Katong and Geylang, and northward along Serangoon Road. By 1843, a road had been cut as far as Bukit Timah, and two years later it reached the Straits of Johore at Kranji, enabling produce from the mainland, previously brought by water, to travel overland. By this time, the physical landscape of the town and harbour had been very considerably changed. Almost the entire length of the harbour had been reclaimed and extended seaward, many hills had been levelled, and few of the town swamps were left undrained. The roads from town to country were bordered by tidal mangrove swamps. Indian *dhobies* or launderers washed clothes all day in the stream running along by the beginning of Orchard Road, as the street named Dhoby Ghaut reminds us. Chinatown had already achieved that extraordinary disorder which now threatens to disappear in urban renewal, having become an ant-heap of shophouses, itinerant foodsellers, opium dens, pavement letter-writers and barbers, sellers of monkeys, birds, shells, coral and cloth, fortune tellers and artisans of all descriptions. By 1861, the seawall, from Johnston's Pier to the Telok Ayer Market, was almost completed. The town itself extended, according to Cameron, in very few points more than a mile from the beach, though Europeans lived as far as four miles out, and in 1868 the road leading north was extended as far as the present Sembawang shipyard, thus opening up the north and north-east.

In the 1880s the roads joining the town and New Harbour were properly established : Anson Road in 1880, Cecil Street and Keppel Road in 1885. Subsequently there was a certain amount of urban development along the fringes of the island's main roads. The building, in 1923, of the causeway to Johore confirmed the importance of the Bukit Timah Road, and, at about the same time, the British naval base formed in the north of the island a nucleus for military personnel, civilian workers, shopkeepers, and those offering services. At the height of its concentration of forces, the British military occupied approximately 15,500 acres, about 11 per cent of Singapore's total land area, in various parts of the island.

Nevertheless, the population remained heavily concentrated round the original settlement in the south-east, and the 1957 census showed maximum gross residential density towards the city centre of over 370,000 persons per square mile. The slums of Chinatown had long been notorious, as a glance at Barrington Kaye's sociological study, *Upper Nankin Street*, will show.

In 1955 Upper Nankin Street, one-eighth of a mile long, and laid out 120 years earlier, had 1,814 people living in its two- and three-storey shophouses. They occupied 465 cubicles, many of them without windows, and 231 bed spaces. The average space per adult was less than 30sq ft, and five of the cubicles were occupied by more than nine people. This population was served by 105 lavatories, all of the open-bucket type, and many of them next to the cooking space.

Housing

In an attempt to wipe out such conditions, the Housing Development Board (HDB) has in recent years provided high-rise flats in the satellite towns of Toa Payoh and Queenstown for the lower-income groups. Queenstown, begun in 1960, contains more than 20,000 units, housing over 110,000 people. When completed it will cover 750 acres and have 27,000 units in all. Toa Payoh, begun in 1965 and due for completion in 1973, will have up to 150,000 persons living in 36,000 units. Housing densities are being made high in order to preserve the catchment area with its reservoirs, parks, golf courses and stretches of secondary forest.

The housing estates, containing one- two- three- and four-room flats, are built on the neighbourhood principle, with schools, markets and shops at groundfloor level, and in some cases clinics and recreational facilities. The government has pursued a deliberate plan of encouraging racial mixture in the allotment of the flats. How far its vast housing programme will succeed in improving the quality of life remains to be seen. Many tenants, previously accustomed to the friendly squalor of Chinatown cubicles, squatter huts or *kampong attap* houses, remain aloof from and suspicious of their neighbours, and a fall from a high-rise block is a frequent method of suicide. Nevertheless, the possible standard of hygiene

31

shows a vast improvement over that of Chinatown and of many *kampongs*.

The kampongs

The *kampong* is a Malay village, originally a cluster of rectangular wooden houses raised from the ground and roofed with *attap*, a thatch made from palm leaves, and set in gardens and groves of fruit trees. As seen in Malaysia, the old-fashioned *kampongs* have great charm, but in Singapore they have assumed a somewhat hybrid character. In some, Chinese, Indians and Malays live side by side, united perhaps by poverty. Many of the *kampongs*, though rural in character, exist well within the city area, where private housing estates have grown up around them. Some are unsightly huddles of shacks made from corrugated iron and old planks. Most are lacking in sanitation, and not all have electricity. The paths of beaten earth between the dwellings become flooded after rain and the settlements present a health hazard, though they are rich in the neighbourliness of the old South East Asia. The steeply raked roofs of the *attap* huts are recalled in the outlines of modern stone buildings such as Singapore's National Theatre, but within the next few decades the *kampong* house itself is likely to become only a memory.

Reclamation

Closely connected with projects of urban renewal is the land reclamation which began in the nineteenth century and had already considerably altered the coastline by 1900. The whole of Collyer Quay was built by reclamation after 1858, and the shoreline of 1843 now runs approximately through the centre of the Padang, across Fullerton Building and along the centre of the buildings standing on the south side of Raffles Place to Finlayson Green. It then continues inland still further and runs just in front of Telok Ayer Street, along to Tanjong Pagar and Keppel Harbour. The Changi swamps were reclaimed in 1927 for defence purposes, and between 1931 and 1936 similar work at Kallang reclaimed 260 acres to provide for Singapore's first civil aerodrome and a harbour for shallow craft. More recently, Queen Elizabeth Walk and the present Nicoll Highway running along the seafront were constructed on reclaimed ground.

Perhaps the most extraordinary work of land transformation is that which took place at Jurong between 1961 and 1966. An area of hills and swamps was changed into an almost level platform in which more than 3,000 acres of land were levelled or reclaimed, and 30 million cubic yd of earth were moved or removed. Bukit Peropok was cut and terraced to form a site for a domestic reservoir. The Jurong coast was extended between 50 and 350ft seawards so that wharves could be built. The reclaimed land became the site for the self-contained town of Jurong, which had a large industrial estate as its nucleus and which by 1980 will have a population of about 70,000. Further reclamation is taking place under the master plan, which is described in Chapter 11.

Buildings

Few of Singapore's old buildings will survive the next decade or so of urban renewal, and few of its inhabitants express regret at the destruction of buildings which, though part of its own history, were set up by foreigners under colonial rule. Those scheduled for preservation include several designed by G. D. Coleman, who lived in Singapore from 1822 to 1844 and designed many of its most attractive buildings. Outstanding among these is the charming Armenian Church which he built in 1835, originally with a dome and bell turret instead of the spire, which dates from 1850.

St Andrew's Cathedral, completed in 1862 on the site of an earlier church, and reputedly given its name because of the number of Scotsmen among the pioneer settlers, will remain. The bell of the old St Andrew's church is in the National Museum, and was presented in 1843 by Mrs Maria Revere Balestier of Boston, Massachusetts, the daughter of Paul Revere by his second

C

marriage, and wife of the first American consul in Singapore. The bell was used at Mrs Revere's insistence to ring the curfew for five minutes each night after a gun was fired at 8pm from Fort Canning. Before 1950, when the only skyscraper in Singapore was the Cathay building, the cathedral and its grassy surroundings, overlooking the Padang—the great stretch of turf with the cricket club at the eastern end—gave a strangely English appearance to this part of central Singapore. Empress Place and the adjacent St Andrew's Road with their impressive white-painted government buildings, some of them constructed round Coleman's designs, recall the days of empire and promote the dignity of independence. For a fuller account of buildings of architectural interest, the reader may refer to Marjorie Doggett's *Characters of Light*, though some of those photographed by her have already been destroyed. One of the most interesting places in Singapore is the old Christian cemetery on Fort Canning, where the ground has been cleared and the gravestones set into the walls. Their inscriptions, with the long catalogue of wives and children lost, of young men dying of tropical disease or disasters at sea, are a poignant reminder of the courage and struggles of the earlier settlers.

Of the outstanding non-European buildings, those scheduled for preservation are mostly *kramats* (Muslim shrines), mosques, and Indian or Chinese temples, some of which are mentioned in Chapter 4. Tan Yeok Neo's house, now used by the Salvation Army, is the last of the four great houses built within a compound in the south Chinese style during the nineteenth century. Its cylindrical roof tiles, surmounted by curling dragons, are worth more than a passing glance.

THE SMALLER ISLANDS

There are some fifty-four offshore islands, of which about two dozen are sizeable and inhabited, and they have a total land area of 14 square miles. The forty-two southern islands are under the administration of a district officer, and the northern and other islands are administered by the commissioner of lands. The most important islands are Tekong Besar, Ubin, Sentosa, and Bukom. It is customary to preface the name with the Malay word *pulau*, meaning 'island'.

Some of the islands are known to have been inhabited by Malays living in *kampongs* built out over the sea on stilts as early as the seventeenth century. Wilde's map of 1680 shows small settlements on Pulau Hantu. Such settlements still exist on several of the islands, notably Telok Saga on Pulau Brani, to the south of Keppel Harbour; it has about 1,300 inhabitants.

With land so short in Singapore, the modern function of each of the islands is carefully planned. The two large islands in the Straits of Johore, to the north-east, Pulau Tekong Besar and Pulau Ubin, will probably be used for agriculture. Pulau Samulon, in the south-west, has been considerably changed in appearance; under the Jurong reclamation scheme, its two hills were levelled, its area increased, and a bridge built to the mainland. Some islands have been taken over for oil installations; they include Pulau Bukom, Pulau Ayer Chawan and Pulau Merlimau. Pulau Blakang Mati, meaning literally, 'island at the back of the dead' was given its new name, Sentosa, which means 'peaceful', when it was singled out at the end of the 1960s for development as a tourist resort.

Several of the islands have been used in the past for military purposes of various kinds, and are the scene of military exercises today. St John's Island, whose name is a corruption of Pulau Sekijang, is now the site of the government Opium Treatment Centre, and a quarantine station for ships, a lazaretto having first been constructed there in 1874. Pulau Brani was for some years under the control of the British military, which has now withdrawn. A naval coal depot and a small repairing dock were built there in the 1860s, and towards the end of the century the Straits Trading Company's smelting plant, still in existence, was established.

One other of Singapore's offshore islands has some claim to fame : Pulau Kusu, almost deserted for the rest of the year, is in October an object of pilgrimage by thousands of Buddhists and Muslims. The Chinese make offerings at the island temple shrine of Toh Peh Kong, the guardian saint of the Overseas Chinese, and the Muslims visit the *kramat* of Dato Syed Abdul Rahman.

3   HISTORY

IT is not known for certain when Singapore was founded. According to the Malay Annals, a Sumatran prince, Sang Nila Utama, saw a lion (probably in fact a tiger) on landing for the first time, founded a settlement and called it Singapura, the city of the lion. The name is derived from the Sanskrit, but it may have been given for religious reasons under Majapahit rule. Some authorities believe Singapura may have been founded about AD 1299.

In 1349 Wang Ta-yuan, a Chinese trader, writes of the Tan-ma-hsi (probably equivalent to Temasek, the old Malay name for the island) alongside which Chinese traders were already settled. He specifically mentions *Lung-ya-men* or 'Dragon Teeth Strait', which lies between Singapore and the island of Sentosa and is now known as Keppel Harbour. According to this account, there were a few barren fields with a little *padi* along the coast, and the place was already notorious for piracy.

The archaeological evidence for the early settlement has vanished, though in 1819 Raffles writes of having noted 'the lines of the old city and its defences' and the 'tombs of the Malay kings' on the hill which is now called Fort Canning. Originally known to the Malays as Bukit Larangan, the Forbidden Hill, Fort Canning is referred to by Wang Ta-yuan as *Pan Tsu*. He writes that it 'rises to a hollow summit, surrounded by interconnected terraces, so that the people's dwellings encircle it'.

Wang's account claims that shorthaired people, with turbans of gold-brocaded satin, and wearing red oiled cloths, lived there

37

under a chieftain, and that the settlement was noted for its fine hornbill casques. The relationship between the people of the hill fortress and the coastal aborigines, the *orang laut* or sea gypsies, remains obscure. Certainly, by the fourteenth century, the island had become involved in the struggle for empire between the Siamese, who were besieging it in the year of Wang's account, and Majapahit, the last Hindu empire of Java. By 1365 it had probably become a dependency of Majapahit, but within a few years fell under the domination of Siam. By the last quarter of the century, the settlement appears to have been utterly destroyed in the conflict between the rival powers.

Singapore's National Museum displays gold ornaments of mid-fourteenth-century Majapahit workmanship, which were dug up in 1928 on Fort Canning. There, too, is to be seen a fragment of the monolith found embedded at the entrance to the Singapore river when the British arrived, and bearing characters in an early Javanese script which may in fact point to a twelfth-century conquest of the island.

Singapura's 'great ruins' were noted by a sixteenth-century Portuguese writer, and there are several references in seventeenth-century Portuguese maps and chronicles to a settlement at this point, but little else is known until Singapore is dramatically recalled to the historical scene in the early nineteenth century.

By then South East Asia had long been the scene of naval and commercial rivalry between the great Christian powers of the West. The first to come were the Portuguese, who captured Malacca, the predominant power in the area, and the local centre for the spread of Islam. In 1596 the first Dutch fleet arrived in South East Asia, in 1602 the Dutch East India Company was formed, and by 1630 the Dutch had gained supremacy in the Spice Islands and the Straits of Malacca. In 1641 they captured Malacca itself.

During the seventeenth century there was fierce rivalry between the Dutch and the English East India Companies for commercial advantage, but after 1623 and the massacre of

Amboina, the British bent all their energies to the struggle with the French for the control of India. The only British settlement remaining in the East after 1685 was Bencoolen, on the west coast of Sumatra. However, the second half of the eighteenth century saw a change in the British attitude when the remarkably rapid growth of trade between India and China drew attention to Malaya and the archipelago. Malaya is almost exactly half-way between India and China. In the days of sailing ships, a landfall on the India-China journey was unavoidable, and any ship on that route was compelled to pass through either the Straits of Malacca or the Straits of Sunda (between Java and Sumatra). For this purpose, Bencoolen was too far from the main trade routes to be effective.

There were other reasons why, after the mid-eighteenth century, the British began to seek a base other than Bencoolen in the area : in order to hold their position in India, they needed a naval repair station on the eastern side of the Bay of Bengal. Commercial advantage spoke too : the goods of India might be exchanged for produce in Malaya and Indonesia of a kind acceptable to the tea merchants of Canton. In this way the necessity of bringing silver from England to pay for China tea was avoided.

The settlement made with these objects in mind at Penang in 1786 proved to be a disappointment, but the British occupied Malacca in 1795, and, using it as a headquarters, accomplished in 1811 the conquest of Java. The man on whose advice and with the aid of whose information the conquest was carried out was Sir Thomas Stamford Raffles.

RAFFLES AND THE BRITISH SETTLEMENT

Raffles was a man of extraordinary abilities and implacable determination. The son of an improvident sea-captain, he was born in 1781, and at fourteen became a clerk at India House, the London office of the East India Company. All his spare time was spent in self-education, and in 1805 he was sent out as assistant secretary to the governor of Penang. Characteristically, he taught himself Malay on the voyage out, and on arrival applied himself to learning everything he could discover about the Malays: their history, languages, customs and traditions, and the fauna and flora of the peninsula. Subsequently he came to the notice of Lord Minto, Governor-General of India, who appointed him as special political agent to the Malay states, and who, after the conquest of Java, made him lieutenant-governor of the territory he had helped to win.

Raffles was a man of his time and a man with a demon: he was convinced that the British had infinitely more to offer the unenlightened than had the Dutch, and the mainspring of his life's work was the attempt to oust the Dutch from their trading monopoly in the archipelago and establish a powerful commercial base, opposing the benefits of free trade to the strangling mesh of Dutch dues and taxes. His dream faded temporarily, as had his hopes of Penang's pre-eminence, when the London Convention of 1814 restored to the Dutch all their former possessions, including Java and Malacca. After an interval spent in England, where he was knighted by George IV, he found himself relegated to the position of lieutenant-governor of Bencoolen. Nevertheless, he wrote at the time, 'I left England under the full impression that I was not only Lieutenant-Governor of Bencoolen, but in fact Political Agent for the Malay States'.

By this time (1818) the Governor-General of India was the Marquess of Hastings, and Raffles paid him a visit, to persuade him to adopt a scheme for establishing 'a station beyond Malacca, such as may command the southern entrance to those Straits'. On his return, Raffles found that Riau, which he and Hastings had fixed on as such a station, had been occupied by the Dutch. Next on the list was Acheh, in the north of Sumatra, but Raffles, ignoring his orders, sailed at once to find a station south of the Straits. Eventually, on 28 January 1819, he landed on Singapore.

At the time, the island had about 150 inhabitants. These included the *orang laut*, presumably descendants of the fishermen and pirates known to be living there in the fourteenth century; about thirty Chinese, some of them gambier planters; and about 100 Malays from Johore who had settled there in 1811, led by the Temenggong, a senior vassal of the sultan.

Two days later, Raffles signed a preliminary agreement with the Temenggong. This had, however, to be ratified by the sultan of Johore, who was under Dutch influence. Since the sultan's claim to power was open to question, Raffles chose to recognise his elder brother Tengku Long as the rightful ruler, and had him brought from Riau to be proclaimed sultan at Singapore. On 6 February an agreement was signed allowing the East India Company to establish a factory, for which Tengku Long was to receive an annual allowance of 5,000 Spanish dollars and the Temenggong one of 3,000. British jurisdiction was to extend from Tanjong Mallang to Tanjong Katong, and as far inland as the range of cannon shot.

Raffles left next day for his post in Bencoolen, returned briefly the same year, and again for a period of eight months between 1822 and 1823. In all, he spent only nine months in the settlement he founded, yet the arrangements he made (and came back to re-inforce when Colonel Farquhar, the first Resident, allowed them to be partly ignored) decided Singapore's future. He died in 1826, of a brain tumour, three of his four children having died in Bencoolen. The East India Company, whose interests, along with those of his country, he had spectacularly served, made unexpected and heavy monetary demands on him in his last years, and harassed his widow until they were paid. Forgotten in England, except perhaps as founder of the London Zoo, he lies buried in Hendon churchyard.

Fortunately Raffles lived long enough to have promise of Singapore's success. At first there was opposition to the settlement, not only from the Dutch but also from various British authorities afraid that Raffles' boldness would provoke Dutch armed attack. However, in March 1824, by the Treaty of London, the Dutch at last recognised the British settlement. In August of the same year a new treaty was negotiated whereby, in return for cash down and pensions for life, the sultan and the Temenggong ceded 'the island of Singapore, together with the adjacent seas, straits and islets, to the extent of ten geographical miles from the coast of the said main island of Singapore'.

In its early years Singapore was a residency controlled from Bencoolen; from 1826 it and Malacca were united to Penang, to form the presidency of the Straits Settlements, under the governor of Penang; and, in 1832, so far had the importance of Singapore mounted beyond that of the other two settlements that it replaced Penang as the seat of government. In 1830, however, the Straits Settlements had been reduced to a mere residency, without their own executive or legislative council, under the governor and council of Bengal. Singapore was therefore controlled from India, and all legislation was passed either by the Indian Legislative Council or by the British Parliament.

The trading settlement prospered at a phenomenal rate. By 1820 its revenue was sufficient to pay for its administration. Its success was due partly to the advantages offered by its vast safe harbour and its central position on the India-China route and for trade with the archipelago, but largely also to the establishment by Raffles from the very start of the principles of free trade and equality before the law. Merchants constrained by Dutch taxes and labourers oppressed by Dutch law were attracted from all parts of the archipelago, and immigrants included Chinese, Malays, Bugis, Javanese, Indians, Thais, Arabs and Armenians. Singapore rapidly became what Raffles, writing in 1818, had sought—'a great commercial emporium and a fulcrum whence we may extend our influence'. He added that 'one free port in these seas must eventually destroy the spell of Dutch monopoly'. So it turned out : the straits were dominated by Penang at one end and by Singapore at the other, and the safety of Britain's China trade was assured.

In the first year or two, a pattern was set that was to endure for over a century : the European merchants controlled the *entrepôt* trade, importing goods from Europe, India and China, and exported the produce of the archipelago, whilst the Chinese acted as agents, collecting the produce of Malaya, Sumatra, Java, and in some cases the neighbouring countries of South East Asia, and passing it on, at a profit, to the European traders. The first junk from China arrived in 1821, sailing before the north-east monsoon, and remaining in port until it could return on the south-west monsoon six months later, bearing a variety of goods, including opium, British cloth, tin, pepper, and edible seaweed. A fleet of Bugis trading ships from the Celebes came in October and November, bearing agar-agar, ebony, camphor and mother-of-pearl. As time went on, Java began to export rice, edible bird's nests, gold dust, indigo, rattans, benjamin, brass, copra, tin, sandalwood, arrack and all manner of spices. From Sumatra came beeswax, coffee, tortoiseshell, rhinoceros horns and elephant tusks. Some of these goods went to Europe, some to Penang and Malacca, some to China. To Java and Sumatra went the goods of India, China and Europe, among them iron, opium, raw silk, wheat, china, ironware, cordage, gunnies and saltpetre, salt, tobacco, firearms, woollens, and porcelain. Later Siam, Cambodia, Brunei and certain of the Malay sultanates were included in this trade.

By 1827 there were in all eighty-seven European males and their families and fourteen European firms in Singapore, most of them agents for London and Calcutta houses. Merchants of out-standing ability, who are commemorated in Singapore street names and whose firms in some instances survive today, had begun to arrive, among them Alexander Guthrie, Alexander Johnston, Edward Boustead, José d'Almeida, Tan Kim Seng, Syed Omar bin Ali Al-junied, the leader of the Arab community, and Naraina Pillai, an Indian who came from Penang. There were also one or two Americans, notably Joseph Balestier, though in the early years US citizens came mostly as missionaries. Merchants and traders used many forms of currency: Dutch guilders, fanams, copper doits, Sicca, Arcot and Java rupees, gold mohurs and

Indian pagodas. The silver Spanish dollar came to be used as the nineteenth-century standard of value.

With such rich cargoes, a cause for concern was the prevalence of piracy. In 1832, despairing of help from the East India Company, a group of Chinese merchants paid for four armed trading boats to defend their vessels. In 1836, after further local pressure, HM sloop *Wolf* arrived to help, followed later by the steamship *Diana*. In her first engagement, six pirate prahus bore down on the *Diana*, under the impression that the smoke from her funnel betokened a sailing ship on fire : they were aghast when she came close up *against the wind* and they found themselves exposed to her guns! Complaints of piracy, however, continued well past the middle of the century, and those taken prisoner by the pirates had their throats cut or were sold into slavery.

In 1834 the British government withdrew the East India Company's monopoly of the Chinese trade, and for some time the trade of Singapore itself declined as a result. However, the European and Chinese merchants were so well established by this time that there was little danger of its continued falling away. In 1837 a chamber of commerce, having both European and non-European members, was founded, and disputed an attempt by the Indian government to impose port duties in Singapore. Their fight succeeded.

Attempts to promote large-scale agriculture were by comparison a failure. The planters of the early years, exclusively Chinese, failed, despite backbreaking work, with cotton, vanilla, gamboge, cinnamon, indigo, cocoa and coffee. Nutmeg, gambier, pepper and sugarcane flourished briefly, but only pineapple and coconut did well.

Gutta percha, the sap of the pertja tree, had long been used by the Malays to make the handles of *parangs* and other implements : it went hard when collected, but was made easily malleable when soaked in hot water. In 1842 a Singapore Malay began to make riding whips of it and sold them to trading ships. Thus brought to the notice of Europeans, gutta percha was sent in

44

small quantities to learned authorities in London and in Calcutta; its uses were subsequently widely developed, and by 1846 it was an important item of Singapore trade and a forerunner of rubber.

THE SECRET SOCIETIES

Little was known of the interior of the island for some decades after the founding of the settlement, and for many years Singapore was virtually a frontier town, with the lawlessness the term implies. Trouble sprang from two interconnected sources in particular: the British rulers' ignorance of Chinese customs and languages, and the prevalence among the Chinese of secret societies, which they had brought with them from their homeland. Not until 1872 did the government employ any Chinese-speaking official. Consequently the Chinese had to be governed by a succession of headmen thrown up from their own numbers and designated 'Captain China'; it is probable that the majority of the Chinese before the 1870s never realised that there was any higher authority in the settlement.

In 1824, the first census ever taken showed a population of 10,683, of whom 3,317 were Chinese, but their numbers increased rapidly, and, with a population increase from 52,891 to 81,734 during the 1850s, the proportion of Chinese rose from 53 per cent to 61 per cent. Almost all were males (in 1850 Chinese men outnumbered women by twelve to one), and most, intending to return eventually to China, had no loyalty to Singapore. Whilst some were ruffians who had left China to escape arrest, most were desperately poor, overworked coolies. For such men, illiterate, unable to speak the language of their British rulers, far from home and hard-pressed in every way, the secret societies were a form of social insurance.

The societies had originated in a seventeenth-century anti-Manchu movement, and the idea was taken up and developed into the triad system in the eighteenth century; the word 'triad' was used to denote that its doctrines were based on the combined

powers of man, earth and heaven. As the secret societies pro-
liferated, various rituals were invented, and members were bound
by scores of stringent regulations. The central idea was that of
'all for one, and one for all', and extreme penalties were exacted
if the group loyalty was betrayed. Each society was confined to
the members of one particular dialect group.

By the 1830s the gambling, opium and toddy monopolies had
been farmed out amongst the Chinese, and in such conditions
there was endless opportunity for the secret societies to make
trouble. The factions representing the different provinces and
dialects of China often fought among themselves, and Tan Che
Sang, the richest of the Chinese merchants in the 1830s, boasted
that he could empty Singapore of all Europeans within a day if
he chose to give the order.

In 1846 there was a bloody street battle when 6,000 Chinese
assembled instead of the 100 given permission by the magistrates
to follow the funeral of the head of one of the secret societies : they
refused to disperse, or to take the route stipulated, and the military
were called out. In 1851 over 500 were killed and twenty-seven
plantations were attacked within a week, in the course of a concerted attack on Roman Catholic converts, the secret societies regarding the Catholic church as a rival society. Three years later
some 600 were killed in riots said to have been sparked off by a
dispute between two Chinese, one a Hokkien and one from Macao,
about the weight of a catty of rice one was selling to the other.
There was more fighting in 1856 and 1863, and by 1858 the
Europeans had made a public complaint.

In 1869, the passing of the Dangerous Societies Suppression
Ordinance, by which all secret societies had to be registered,
proved completely ineffectual, and there were two serious riots
caused by rivalry between the Hokkien and Teochew in 1871.
But in 1872 Walter Pickering, a fluent Chinese speaker,
arrived to act as official interpreter. One of the first things he did
was to alter the notices of government decisions posted by the
Chinese headmen, who, unknown to the British, had been de-

scribing their colonial rulers as 'red-haired barbarians', 'devils', or, in the case of the police, 'big dogs'.

In 1876, the posts of Protector of Chinese Immigrants and Protector of Chinese Emigrants were set up and combined in the person of Pickering, in an attempt to bring the Chinese in closer touch with the reality of British rule and to weaken the power of the secret societies. An Act of Suppression was put into force in 1890, but for the most part the societies simply went underground, and up to the present time have continued to cause trouble in varying degrees at various times.

DOMESTIC LIFE

In the early years, the houses in Singapore had been wooden bungalows roofed with *attap*, the streets muddy tracks subject to flooding, and there were no bridges, only a ferry across the Singapore river. By the 1860s many Europeans lived in brick bungalows set in 10 or 15 acres of garden, their inside walls painted white, their floors matted, and the rooms divided by silken screens set on hinges. Clusters of argand lamps hung from the ceilings, and in the dining-rooms punkahs were kept in motion as vast formal dinners, consisting of several substantial courses, with the addition of curry and rice, were consumed.

For many years, everyone woke to the sound of the gun shot off at 5am from the slopes of Fort Canning. The men, Cameron tells us, rose to walk or ride for an hour or two in the cool of the morning; after which they lolled about in *baju* and pyjamas for some time, drinking tea or writing letters; and presently retired to the bathroom, where, in lieu of what is known in modern Singapore as a 'long-bath', they poured cold water over themselves from a huge Shanghai jar. Later they rode into town to their offices, picking up the latest gossip in Commercial Square before beginning work. 'Tiffin-time' was one o'clock, and by four-thirty or so the men were ready to play fives or cricket at the Esplanade ground.

Twice a week the ladies and children drove in their carriages to attend the musical evenings, when a regimental or naval band played on the Esplanade until half-past six : on particularly dark nights, syces ran beside the horses with lanterns on the homeward journey.

Cameron writes that in 1865 there were 'not over forty families who aim to form a part of society' and hints that they were over-restrictive in admitting newcomers to their circle. Any suggestion of Indian descent, he said, was 'an insuperable impediment', and ladies had been known to refuse to dance opposite others whose complexion was thought suspiciously sallow.

Dinner parties, occasional balls and amateur theatrical entertainments varied the monotony of domestic life, but the womenfolk must have spent much of their time dealing with regiments of servants. Low, writing of life in the early 1840s, declared that for 'a moderate family' the usual tally was two underservants, one maid, one tailor, one cook and his assistant, one washerman, two grooms, one grasscutter, one lamplighter and sweeper, one scavenger and one waterman.

Several writers, Raffles among them, hint that the minds of European women in Singapore were obsessively occupied with questions of precedence on public occasions. Meantime, the life of the other races who inhabited Singapore remained almost unknown to them, though a daring compatriot, Mrs Florence Candy, in the course of a tour on the Duke of Sutherland's yacht, visited a rich Chinese living near the catchment area in the 1880s, and wrote that :

> he has . . . open-worked traceries screens painted in white and pale porcelain colours all over his house as partitions to the rooms, with the few solid wall spaces hung with the Japanese pictures called Kakemonos, making the whole house one veiled aerial perspective set with flowers all about the open courts and pathways. Here he sits in azure silk raiment, and amuses himself and his friends with fishing for fat carp from his windows and feeding them with dozens of slices of bread.

Page 49 Sir Thomas Stamford Raffles, founder of modern Singapore, from a portrait of 1817 by Joseph, in the National Portrait Gallery, London

Page 50 Vision and reality: *(above)* the Padang in 1851, from an oil painting by J. T. Thomson: a somewhat romanticised view of Singapore life; *(below)* harsh reality: Chinese cake-sellers in the 1880s. Portable stoves like the one left of centre are still used by hawkers

THE CHINESE CITY

In 1845 came the opening of steamship communication between
Europe and the Straits Settlements. At first there was little commercial advantage : passengers and mail took the overland route
between the Red Sea and the Mediterranean, but most cargo
still came round the Cape of Good Hope by sail. Ships rounding
the Cape often bypassed Singapore, going through the Straits
of Sunda instead of the Straits of Malacca. The balance was re-
dressed in 1852, when, following the Australian gold rush, the
new P & O run from Singapore to Australia was inaugurated.
Singapore was now more than a convenient stop between India
and China : it was becoming the centre of a worldwide web of
communication, and the opening of the Suez Canal in 1869
confirmed its importance.

In the first four or five decades of its existence, Singapore had
been a small settlement on the edge of a jungle-covered, tiger-
infested island, inhabited by a miscellaneous collection of races
following a variety of religions, the whole loosely cobbled into
order by British law administered from India, local headmen
and secret societies, and bound effectively by the two things held
in common : the desire to make money and the recognition that,
if anyone rocked the golden boat too hard, they might all be
tipped out.

By the last third of the century, Singapore, now predominantly
Chinese in population, had become the centre of distribution of
labour throughout the British and Dutch territories in the area,
and the commercial capital of the Overseas Chinese. This was
a result partly of the upswing of world trade at this period,
causing an unprecedented demand for labour, and partly of
increasingly troubled conditions in China. The Malays, never
the commercially active sector of the population, lacked the incentive to compete with the Chinese, who increased and multiplied and prospered. In 1878 there were 34,000 Chinese
immigrants; in 1888, 103,000. Between 1871 and 1881 the

D

population of Singapore rose by 43 per cent, from 97,111 to 139,208.

Encouraged to shrewdness and independence of mind by their calling, the European and Chinese merchants joined forces to protect Singapore's interests. In 1855 they successfully protested against the Indian Currency Act, which threatened to replace the silver dollar currency with Indian rupees. In 1857, a public meeting supported the plea of the Calcutta merchants for direct government, and proposed to ask the same for Singapore itself.

In 1858 Queen Victoria became the head of the Indian Empire, and the East India Company's control was abolished. But it was not until 1867 that Singapore was placed under the direct government of the secretary of state at the Colonial Office, London, and a separate Malay civil service was established. A governor was appointed, advised by an executive committee comprising senior officials, and a legislative council which included a number of nominated unofficials chosen from among the leading merchants. The first Asian unofficial, Hoo Ah Kay, known as 'Whampoa', was appointed in 1871; he was at that time almost the only Chinese who spoke English with any fluency, and a famous Singapore character.

In 1873, the Singapore *Daily Times* remarked that financial stability had improved since the change of government, but complained nevertheless of the

> woeful, and seemingly wilful, neglect, if not worse, of urgent public works, the hasty, precipitate legislation, the persistent and contemptuous disregard of public opinion, insolence and positive neglect of duty on the part of Public Officials, the needless centralisation of power in Singapore to the loss and irritation of Malacca and Penang, the incessant changes of Officials in most Public Departments, suspicion of the integrity and independence of magistrates, the continuous increase of Establishments without any equivalent, the unsatisfactory constitution of the Police, and lastly as well as finally, the utter powerlessness of the community, the taxpayers, to have their views and wishes carried out or listened to.

Discontent crystallised round the failure to produce waterworks, even after fourteen years of talk and a donation for the purpose from a wealthy Chinese citizen, and round the 'railway scandal'. This involved the plan to construct a railway from the town to the wharves, which it was agreed by the legislative council should be constructed by a private company. The decision not to use public money for the scheme was reversed by the Colonial Office in 1872, and led to a public protest meeting against the principle of 'the Colonial Office entering upon any scheme entailing large expenditure of the revenue of the colony without the sanction of the Local Legislature'. The dispute dragged on until 1874, and in the end no railway was constructed.

Often pulling against such interference in local affairs, the Singapore merchants sometimes attempted also to push the London authorities into action, notably in the question of intervention in the Malay States. Unsettled conditions, and strife between local Malay rulers and leaders of Chinese labour, encouraged by Siamese interference, threatened to disrupt trade in Malaya and cause heavy losses in Singapore. In 1873 the Chinese merchants petitioned for British intervention to restore order, and between 1871 and 1877, steps were taken which left Perak and the west coast of the peninsula firmly in British hands : another factor in Singapore's continuing growth and prosperity had been stabilised. In 1895 the Federation of Malay States was placed under the authority of the resident-general in Kuala Lumpur, and he in turn was made responsible to the governor of the Straits Settlements at Singapore in his capacity as high commissioner for Malaya. The four northern Malay States were transferred to the British in 1909, and British sway over Malayan territory was complete when Johore came under its control in 1914.

About the turn of the century, immense new sources of wealth opened for Malaya and thus for Singapore, and after 1900 the island became the world centre of tin and rubber distribution. In the 1880s the meat-canning industry had begun in the USA.

The Straits Trading Company built a smelter at Pulau Brani in 1890, and by 1895 was producing one-third of the total Malayan production of tin. About this time Henry Ridley, from 1888 director of the Singapore Botanical Gardens, succeeded, after years of struggle, in persuading the Chinese to sow rubber seeds from London's Kew Gardens on Malacca plantations, and invented a commercially profitable tapping process. Thus was Malaya's greatest source of income initiated and, with political stability now established in the western Malay States, the flow of Singapore capital into tin mining and rubber planting markedly increased.

The new industries attracted thousands of Chinese and Indians, who worked the tin mines and rubber plantations respectively, using Singapore as their jumping-off point. As yet, very few Indians willingly remained for long away from India, but as the century advanced the Singapore Chinese began to form a genuine community. Although for the most part these Chinese were married to women of Malay extraction, and spoke Malay rather than Chinese, new developments in China roused a feeling of nationalism and confirmed their cultural identity. There had been no protest and little sign of interest among the Singapore Chinese when, from 1839 to 1842, British troops used Singapore as a base to fight the Chinese in the opium wars, but in 1900 $100,000 (£13,600; US $33,300) was collected in Singapore to finance an anti-Manchu revolt in China. In the next few years, many risings were similarly financed, and Kang Yu Wei and Sun Yat Sen, revolutionary leaders, visited Singapore on proselytising missions. It was about this time that the distinction between China-born and Straits-born Chinese became more obvious, as the latter grew numerous and wealthy enough to form a distinct community.

By the 1920s, many middle-class Chinese families in Singapore were speaking Mandarin and their womenfolk had reverted to Chinese costume and hairstyles. Side by side with pride in their traditional culture went a loyalty, sometimes tasting oddly of

54

sycophancy or cultural displacement, to Britain, many of them having, no doubt for reasons of convenience, become British subjects.

In 1900 the Straits Chinese British Association was formed, with loyal and patriotic motives, and in 1901 the first Eurasian and Chinese companies of the volunteer infantry were established. The Straits Chinese Recreation Club, which followed all the main European athletic pursuits, had existed since 1885. The early twentieth-century mission schools, mostly Roman Catholic or Methodist, which taught in English, led to a division between the Chinese-educated Chinese and the English-educated Chinese which was to have considerable importance in mid-twentieth-century politics.

SINGAPORE, 1900–42

Singapore continued in general to prosper until the depression of the thirties. In 1903 the Kwong Yik Bank was set up as the first banking institution run by the Chinese. In 1906 the Chinese Chamber of Commerce was established, and in the same year the Straits dollar, with fixed parity, was introduced. In 1911 the Singapore Chamber of Commerce Rubber Association was established, and rubber might thenceforth be bought and sold on the spot instead of on the London Rubber Market as it was previously.

World War I touched Singapore relatively lightly : some 10,000 Chinese were voluntarily repatriated under a government scheme when the war caused unemployment, and in 1915 came the brief, abortive mutiny of part of a regiment of Indian troops, possibly encouraged by German propaganda. Planes and tanks were paid for by wealthy Chinese individuals as their loyal contribution to the war effort, but Malaya as a whole was very little affected, since, of the great powers, France and Japan were allies, there were no German bases nearby, and the Dutch remained neutral.

By 1916, Japan was in control of the China Seas, yet at the time of the 1921 conference on naval disarmament, Britain declined to renew the Anglo-Japanese alliance, first created in

1902 to enable Britain to concentrate her naval power against the Germans in the west. Unwilling to face the expense of supporting a second, Far East, fleet, Britain compromised by deciding on a naval base to be constructed in Singapore, reasoning that the fleet could be moved east in the event of attack from that quarter. The construction of the base was interrupted several times during the 1920s, following the fluctuations of government in Britain, but in February 1938 the naval dockyard was opened, still without plans for a fleet of its own. The coast facing Malaya remained totally undefended, as it was assumed that Indochina and France would remain friendly and that attack could come only from the sea.

In the interwar period, Singapore became, for Europeans, the self-sufficient, slightly unreal, curiously isolated society depicted in the stories of Somerset Maugham : a distribution and leave centre for the lonely planters of the mainland, and a city where the British reigned unchallenged and the Eurasians dwelt, economically and socially, in a no-man's-land. As for European treatment of the other races, it is instructive to note that Roland Braddell, in *The Lights of Singapore*, published in 1934, implores his readers not to hit or kick their rickshaw boy, 'as I too often see people doing'. Economically, Singapore was affected by the depression, and in 1932 the Aliens' Ordinance, seeking to prevent further unemployment and the racial tensions that might arise from it, forbade the immigration of males. The result was to encourage the immigration of women, the proportion of whom among the Chinese rose from 18 per cent in 1911 to 44 per cent in 1947, and to stabilise the population considerably.

THE OCCUPATION

The fall of Singapore was considered by many to be the greatest British military disaster in history. Ironically, the island's life was barely touched in the first two years of war. Then came the rapid Japanese land advance from South Thailand and North Malaya, following the attack on Pearl Harbour, on 8 December 1941; the bombing of British airfields in the north of the peninsula, the sinking of two British battleships, and Japanese air raids over and shelling of Singapore from the mainland. The enemy troops had reached the southern tip of Malaya within a few weeks, helped by their own careful prewar preparations and by the lack of air cover on the British side. The two battleships, *Prince of Wales* and *Repulse*, sent ahead without air support as tokens of the Far East fleet the British lacked, were bombed and sunk on 10 December. The heavy guns protecting Singapore faced south, and were useless against the Japanese attack. Winston Churchill, discovering this state of affairs from Lord Wavell, the first allied supreme commander of the war, a month before Singapore fell, commented that 'the possibility of Singapore having no landward defences no more entered my mind than that of a battleship being launched without a bottom'.

British and Australian troops fought bravely, but their commanders were taken by surprise, unsupported by air or sea. On 31 January the British army fell back across the Causeway into Singapore. General Yamashita, in command of the Japanese forces, later wrote that his troops were outnumbered three to one, and that a long period of street fighting might well have resulted in his defeat.

Yamashita launched his assault during the night of 8 February, having landed 3,000 men on the island. The naval base had been abandoned even before the army had retreated as far as Singapore. There was a lack of co-ordination between the services, and a complete absence of plan for the evacuation of key personnel. The result was chaos, and on 15 February the British GOC, Lieutenant-General A. E. Percival, signed an unconditional surrender in the Ford motor factory at Bukit Timah.

Singapore was occupied by the Japanese until September 1945. Their avowed aim was to establish the 'Greater East Asia Co-Prosperity Sphere', and the idea behind this was to build up an economic system independent of the rest of the world, with

Japan as its nucleus. Singapore was singled out as the capital of the sphere's southern region, and was intended to become the chief military supply base in the area. It was renamed *Syonan*, or 'Brilliant South'. The Japanese military administration was ordered to acquire and control all possible economic resources towards the prosecution of the war; the city was expected to become self-sufficient in food and daily necessities. The Japanese military headquarters was set up in the Cathay Building in Dhoby Ghaut.

Those white civilians who had not been able to escape by air or boat were lined up on the Padang and marched off to Changi jail with what belongings they could carry or push along with their children in prams. The prisoners were until August 1942 allowed to organise themselves under their own administration; after that they came under direct Japanese control. In 1944 the civilians were moved from Changi jail to Sime Road to make way for the POWs, who were taken there from the Selarang Barracks at Changi. The conditions prevailing in Changi jail in the later years of the occupation are vividly described in Russell Braddon's *The Naked Island*, which has contemporary illustrations by the cartoonist Ronald Searle, who ran the camp magazine; and, in fictionalised form, in James Clavell's *King Rat*.

In the first three days of the occupation thousands of Chinese were rounded up so that the Japanese could dispose of the 'anti-Japanese elements' among them. These included anyone suspected of having supported the mainland Chinese by word or deed in the Sino-Japanese struggle. Those picked out were driven away to the beaches, where they were shot in their thousands. For the rest, many of whom found that their houses had been looted by Japanese soldiers or by other sections of the population in their absence, the struggle to live began.

At the beginning of the occupation, many people were thrown out of work when European firms closed down, and for the rest there were cuts in salary, sometimes amounting to half. People were urged to take up vegetable and poultry farming, and the tennis courts attached to the former residences of the wealthy were dug up for vegetable plots, but the produce was often carried off by the army with no or inadequate payment. Many people sold their belongings until they had nothing left to sell.

The looting of the early days diminished suddenly after the Japanese had publicly executed some of the offenders and exhibited their heads on pikes, but the looted goods found their way on to the market and fetched high prices from the Japanese themselves. Price control was then introduced, but failed to prevent constantly growing inflation, which was exacerbated by the excessive issue of Japanese military scrip, known as 'banana' notes. The price of a hen's egg rose from two cents in December 1941 to $10 (£1·35; US $3·3) in June 1945; the value of a Parker fountain pen rose in the same period from $15 (£2; US $5) to $5,000 (£680; US $1,666) and that of a piano from $200 (£27·25; US $66) to $15,000 (£2,000; US $5,000). As time went on, medicine as well as food became desperately short, though items of both kinds were exhibited for sale at black market prices to 'Nippon-zin' only.

The struggle to survive made each man distrust his neighbour. Some, desperate for money, became police informers; others resorted to blackmail, playing on the universal fear of the secret police, the Kempeitai. As Tan Thoon Lip puts it in his account of the occupation, 'You had only to breathe "communist" of a person and that person would disappear, none would dare say a word in his favour, much less defend him.' The Orchard Road YMCA became notorious as the headquarters of the Kempeitai and its torturers, and there are many eyewitness accounts of the terrifying brutalities that were commonplace.

From July 1942, every family was registered with the police and the families were formed into teams of thirty with a headman appointed from amongst themselves. Ten teams constituted a ward, and ten wards an area, and each of the seven areas coincided with a police division. In this way, control was exercised over the populace, and each man might be held responsible for the behaviour of his fellows. Another way in which the people were controlled was through the rationing of rice : in order to encourage co-operation with the conquerors, supplementary rations were given to government and municipal employees, and a higher ration still to employees of the military.

The Japanese did not treat all the sections of the community alike. A 'loyal donation' of $50 million (£6,800,000; US $17 million) was exacted from Malayan Chinese and collected in Singapore through the Overseas Chinese Association, which was formed at the instance of the Japanese immediately after the massacre in the first week of the occupation. It was made to organise meetings and mass rallies calling for co-operation with the Japanese, and was required to help maintain law and order.

The Eurasians and Indians were, each in a different way, accorded special attention. Eurasian support for the 'Greater East Asia Co-Prosperity Sphere', which the Japanese claimed to be establishing, was sought and to some extent obtained : the Eurasians, like the rest, were told that the Japanese had rescued them from the European yoke, but were left in no doubt as to what would happen if they failed to co-operate. As in other territories they had occupied, the Japanese encouraged Indian nationalist aspirations and the formation of an Indian nationalist army. Subhas Chandra Bose, the leading Indian nationalist, was flown in, and in fact was the first to proclaim the existence of an independent India, at a meeting in the Cathay Building.

Japanese propaganda had some success with the population at large, particularly in the form of radio, and newsreel and educational films. The press was taken over, and the prohibition of shortwave radio sets meant that only Japanese propaganda could be heard. All former English schools were converted into a system of primary common public schools, and the vernacular primary schools were allowed to continue; but the high schools were not reopened until March 1945, and then only two of them. The school curriculum throughout the occupation consisted largely of Japanese language lessons, physical training and vegetable gardening. All pupils sang the Japanese national anthem and bowed towards the north-east each morning.

The Victoria Hall clock was changed to Tokyo time; the statue of Raffles was put into store, to be sent to Japan for melting down when the moment of final victory should come; a victory memorial was built in Bukit Timah Road, and a Fuji Regiment memorial and an elaborate shrine in the MacRitchie reservoir area. There was little news of the outside world—so little, that when the British returned in 1945 few understood why rationing continued and conditions remained difficult, and the resulting disillusionment with British rule grew even stronger.

The occupation had certain longterm effects. The Changi prisoners were made to build an airfield, on which flying operations began in 1944, and the Japanese extended the civil airport at Kallang almost as far as Tanjong Katong Road. There was considerable deforestation, both by the Japanese and by local people in the desperate search for fuel. Immigration came to a halt for three and a half years, stabilising the population still further. The housing shortage worsened, and urban squatter *kampongs* spread unchecked. The occupation left a legacy of starvation, beri-beri, malaria, TB and VD, and at its end there was chaos. The Japanese surrendered three weeks before the British forces arrived, and the interim saw an orgy of thieving, looting, violent acts of personal revenge, and a spending spree in an attempt to get rid of Japanese currency. For a short time, barter replaced money transactions. There were few vehicles left on the streets except for the trishaw and the obsolescent rickshaw. The gas for street lighting had failed months before the British return, and most of the public utilities were in badly kept condition. The local population was swollen by numbers of displaced persons, especially Javanese, living in severe deprivation. By the end of 1945, large numbers of white Dutch in transit from Indonesia added to the pressure on services.

After 208 days of British military administration, the civilian government resumed charge on 1 April 1946. That the British would again take over the government of Singapore was naturally assumed by their own people; it was not so obvious an outcome in the minds of the local populace. Some thought Singapore might be handed over to the nationalist government to become a part of China, the only Asian victor on the allied side. Others felt it might be absorbed as part of an *Indonesia Raya* or *Malaysia Raya*—the Greater Indonesia or Malaysia towards which many Malays in South East Asia had planned for some time. Others wondered whether Singapore would be taken over by local Chinese communists, whose underground forces had, in conjunction with the British, been foremost in defending the mainland against the Japanese, and who might well have been prepared to kill the re-occupying British forces in pursuit of their aims.

Nevertheless, the most important result of the British defeat and the Japanese occupation was the overthrowing in the minds of the local people of the image of British supremacy and invulnerability, though, as in other colonial dominions, it was only a matter of time before independence must be granted. Plans made by Whitehall long before the end of the war consistently treated Singapore and Malaya as separate entities, and on the resumption of civil administration in 1946, Singapore was made a crown colony, together with the Cocos and Christmas Islands; though the relevant white paper declared it was no part of the British government's policy 'to preclude or prejudice in any way the fusion of Singapore and the Malayan Union in a wider union at a later date should it be considered that such a course were desirable'.

Prewar opportunities for participation in government had been practically non-existent. At the time of the fall of Singapore, the unofficial members of the legislative council were nominated by the governor on a racial basis : 5 Europeans, 3 Chinese British subjects, 1 Indian British subject, 1 Malay and 1 Eurasian; and by the chamber of commerce. The constitution had remained fundamentally unchanged since 1867. The executive council was not responsible to the legislative council and could reject its advice, and the governor called and prorogued the legislative council, initiated most legislation, and assented to or vetoed all bills, at his discretion. Government was thus essentially by the governor, who was subject only to the control of the Secretary of State for the Colonies at Whitehall. This state of affairs continued virtually unchanged until the introduction of the Rendel Constitution in 1955, although in the first postwar elections, in March 1948, six of the twenty-one members of the legislative council were chosen by popular ballot. The franchise was, however, extremely limited, being confined to British subjects over twenty-one and of at least one year's residence. The number of elected members, including chamber of commerce appointees, rose to twelve in the 1951 election. Only 52 per cent of the registered voters troubled to visit the polls.

The Rendel Constitution, introduced in April 1955, provided for twenty-five elected members out of a legislative assembly of thirty-two; but the franchise was kept for British subjects, and pressure to make Chinese an official language failed. The executive council was replaced by a council of nine ministers, six of them recommended from the legislative assembly by their most obvious leader, and was made largely responsible for internal affairs. The three others, appointed by the governor, were responsible for external affairs, defence and security. The chambers of commerce lost their seats. The Labour Front, led by David Marshall, a Jewish lawyer, won ten seats and formed a government with the support of the Alliance party, the trade unions and students. At the first meeting of the assembly, Lee Kuan Yew, one of the three People's Action Party (PAP) candidates returned, made a fiery speech in which he declared, 'This constitution is colonialism in disguise'.

The Labour Front government was plagued by strikes and unrest in schools and unions. Ever since the end of the war, strikes and communist-led agitators had bedevilled the economy. One result was that the government was at last compelled to consult with non-English-speaking pressure groups.

In April 1956 an all-party mission to the United Kingdom, seeking independence for Singapore, failed : the British were unwilling to give up the right of ultimate control. Marshall resigned, and in October 1956 there were outbreaks of arson and serious student riots, in some of which the PAP (in which communists were rapidly gaining control) was involved. Of thirty-five communists arrested as security risks in 1957, sixteen were PAP members. Later the PAP revised its system of membership to keep communists out of responsible posts.

Internal self-government was finally agreed on in 1958, Britain retaining control over defence and external affairs, and in May 1959 the PAP won forty-three out of fifty-one seats and 53·4 per cent of the votes. Lee Kuan Yew, now acknowledged leader of the party, became prime minister, and on 3 June the new State of Singapore came into being. (The Cocos Islands had been put under Australian administration in 1955, and Christmas Island now followed them.) On 3 December the first local Head of State, Inche Yusof bin Ishak, was installed, replacing Sir William Goode, the last colonial governor.

MERGER

The first years of power were difficult and unsettled for the new government. In 1960 Lee's leadership was challenged by Ong Eng Guan, the party's treasurer, and the issue was settled in Lee's favour only with communist support. In 1961, however, the growing conflict between leftwing and moderate elements in the PAP came into the open on the issue of merger with Malaya, and in July the party rebels, led by the communist Lim Chin Siong, walked out of the assembly after the government had in principle agreed to merger. They formed a new party, the Barisan Sosialis, and the government had to rely on the temporary support of the United Malay National Organisation (UMNO) and the Singapore People's Alliance to make up for its loss of an overall majority. Some observers believe that the PAP lost as much as 80 per cent of its membership in 1961; it was only the tactical skill and tenacity of its leaders which saved it from extinction.

The question of merger with Malaya had been a key consideration since the return of the colonial government to Singapore. The British, having stampeded the sultans of the Malayan states into agreeing to a Malayan union in which their own power would be ceded to the British, and people of other races with a certain length of residence would have equal citizenship rights with the Malays, planned in 1946 to appoint a governor-general to oversee the work of the governors of the Malayan Union and Singapore respectively. Pan-Malayan aspects of administration were to include currency, higher education, immigration, income tax, civil aviation, posts and telegraphs, and shipping. Singapore was to be a separate crown colony, not only for military and economic reasons (Singapore depended on trade, whereas Malaya drew three-fifths of her revenue from customs duties) but also because of Malay fears of Chinese dominance. The 1947 census showed that in Malaya-with-Singapore, the proportion of Chinese was 45 per cent and that of the Malays themselves only 43·3 per cent. In Malaya separated from Singapore, the proportions were roughly reversed, the rest being Indians.

The Chinese had long been pre-eminent in Malayan economic life, and the hostility produced as a result of their commercial success was exacerbated by the fact that few were converts to Islam. There was extremely strong Malay opposition to the idea of equal citizenship for the various races, and to the transfer of power from the sultans, who are still widely venerated.

The Malayan Union was scrapped almost immediately, and in its place came a federation, set up on 1 February 1948, in which

65

citizenship laws for non-citizens were made more stringent, the sultans retained their power, and the British high commissioner was charged with safeguarding the special position of the Malays.

Nevetheless, although there were serious difficulties in the way of merger between Singapore and Malaya, many people continued to look to it as an inevitable development of the future. On taking power in 1959, Lee Kuan Yew declared that internal selfgovernment for Singapore was 'but a step towards *Merdeka* (freedom) and merger'.

The Emergency

The position had been complicated by the Emergency declared by the British authorities in Malaya on 16 June 1948. This was a result of intense guerrilla activity by the remnants of communist forces, largely Chinese, which had formed the nucleus of the Malayan People's Anti-Japanese Army and fought alongside the British, and which, though in part disarmed and disbanded after the war, fought on with a view to taking over Malaya piece by piece and uniting it with Singapore. The Emergency became much more acute at the beginning of 1950, and Lee Kuan Yew, then a law student, addressing a meeting in London, stated that 'the continued existence of the new Asiatic States depends upon whether they are able to carry out long overdue reforms; whether they can, without the communist religion, do all the communist state can do for the masses'. He went on to point out that the first problem in his own part of the world was that of racial harmony between Chinese and Malays, and the second the formation of a united political front strong enough to demand full independence from the British. In the first postwar decade, the interdependence of these aims was clearly demonstrable.

General Sir William Templer gradually brought the Emergency under control during the early fifties, and it was declared ended in 1960, Malaya having already been granted independence in August 1957. But the growing leftwing agitation in

Page 67 Modern Singapore: *(above)* aerial view of the Singapore River. The Padang and St Andrew's Cathedral are on the left; *(below)* boats at Boat Quay, with shophouses top left

Page 68 Contrasting people of nineteenth-century Singapore: *(above)* a Muslim family; the man on the left and two of the boys wear the Malay *songkok*; the man in the tarboosh is probably Indian; *(below)* Indian pedlars; their descendants may be among Singapore's many wealthy textile merchants

Singapore which characterised the late fifties made the Malayan
Federation less than ever keen on merger. Having put down their
own communists after a long struggle, they were not anxious to
import further sources of trouble from Singapore. The leftwing
elements in Singapore were themselves against merger by this
time, evidently fearing suppression by the combined powers of
the Malayan Federation and Singapore.

The prime ministers of Malaya and Singapore were, however,
whatever their differences, determined to oust the communists,
and the final showdown in the Singapore Parliament and the
formation of the Barisan Sosialis party by the PAP rebels, already
referred to, came in July 1961, the same month in which a
regional conference of Malaya, Singapore, North Borneo, Brunei
and Sarawak declared itself in favour of a merger of all the territories taking part. The PAP rebels had hoped to take over by
appealing to the largely Chinese electorate in Singapore on the
twin issues of immediate and complete selfgovernment, and a
refusal of the proposed regional merger in which the Chinese
would not be numerically dominant, as they would be in a union
between Singapore and the federation only. Lee Kuan Yew and
the loyalists having managed to retain power by the skin of their
teeth, Lee and the Malayan Prime Minister, Tunku Abdul
Rahman, announced their agreement in principle to merger,
which was subsequently accepted by Britain, subject to her
retaining her Singapore military bases.

In September 1962 a referendum on the merger was held in
Singapore : voters—144,077 of whom cast blanks, as suggested
by the Barisan Sosialis—voted only on the terms proposed, not
on the desirability of merger itself. Seventy-one per cent voted
for the terms proposed by the government, according to which
Singapore gave up control over foreign affairs, defence and
security to the central government in Kuala Lumpur, but retained
its powers over finance, labour and education. Singapore was to
have fifteen seats out of 159 in the federal legislature, but was to
retain its own parliamentary assembly, executive government,

and *Yang di-pertuan Negara* (head of state). Singapore was to keep 60 per cent of its revenue, and it was agreed that in due course a customs union and a common market should be created. Lee Kuan Yew declared Singapore's de facto independence on 31 August 1963, the date originally set for the establishment of Malaysia : the prime minister of Malaya deferred implementing the Malaysia agreement for another two weeks because of objections by President Sukarno of Indonesia.

SEPARATION

Major causes of friction between Singapore and Malaysia soon became apparent : they included financial and economic disputes, disagreements over the control of Singapore's defence bases and facilities, and widely separated views on matters of general policy.

In the Singapore general election of September 1963 the PAP won 47 per cent of the votes and thirty-seven seats and the Barisan Sosialis 32·1 per cent and thirteen seats, the leftwing being split by the newly-formed United People's Party. The constitution was changed so that any assemblyman resigning or being expelled lost his seat and could not change sides. In the Malaysian general election of 1964, the PAP won one seat and this, plus the existing Singapore-held seats, made it the largest single opposition group in the Malayan Parliament. The wisdom of merger subsequently came into question more urgently in Malayan minds.

The merger had already been characterised by President Sukarno of neighbouring Indonesia as a 'neo-colonialistic plot' and on 20 January 1963 he declared the policy of *konfrontasi* (armed confrontation).

Nineteen sixty-four was a year of unrest, including strikes, student demonstrations, and attempts by Indonesian saboteurs to blow up Merdeka Bridge and the watermain bringing water across the Causeway. The culmination was the outbreak of the Singapore race riots of 21 July and 2 September 1964, in which

70

varying estimates give 21–31 dead, and 460–600 injured. There were 1,700 arrests. On 5 September the whole of Malaysia was declared a security area, and Singapore a danger zone.

In May 1965, the PAP delegates and the opposition parties of the states of Malaya and the Borneo territories signed a declaration of the Malaysian Solidarity Convention appealing for an end to communal politics and using the slogan 'A democratic Malaysian Malaysia'. Combined with Malay dissatisfaction with the PAP and the Chinese in general over questions such as employment and educational opportunities, housing and land reservation, this was the last straw for rightwing extremists in the Malayan Alliance Party. With pressure to imprison the PAP leaders mounting, Tunku Abdul Rahman, the Malaysian Prime Minister, issued a statement on 5 August 1965 making it clear that Singapore must withdraw. The separation agreement was made on 7 August 1965, and Singapore's full independence as a sovereign state was declared on 9 August. *Konfrontasi* came to an end, and later Singapore resumed full diplomatic relations with Indonesia. In 1965 she became a member both of the British Commonwealth of Nations and of the United Nations.

In October 1966, all Barisan Sosialis assemblymen resigned, and the party declared it was changing its strategy from 'parliamentary struggle' to 'mass struggle outside parliament' in which it would rely on rallies and house-to-house campaigns. Parliament assured the public that it would assume 'the responsibility of the opposition to examine all measures tabled by the government'. At the 1968 election, boycotted by the Barisan Sosialis, the PAP won all seats, thus bearing out the campaign speech of Mr S. Rajaratnam, the Foreign Minister, in which he said 'the people are more interested in what is good government than in having an opposition'.

In 1967 the British Defence White Paper made it clear that Britain would withdraw entirely from the Singapore bases by the mid-1970s; the date was later put forward to the end of 1971, and the extent of the withdrawal was scaled down, but it brought

71

new problems, both economic and military, for the Singapore government.

Symbols of State

The flag of Singapore, halved horizontally, is red over white. At the top of the hoist is a crescent moon sided by five stars in a circle, all in white. The colour red signifies the universal brotherhood and equality of man, and the colour white symbolises purity and virtue. The crescent represents a young country on the ascent, and the five stars signify democracy, peace, progress, justice and equality.

The arms of Singapore consist of a shield on which is emblazoned a white crescent moon and five white stars on a red background. Supporting the shield is a lion on the left, representing Singapore, and a tiger on the right, representing the island's links with Malaya. Below the shield is a banner bearing the republic's motto *Majulah Singapura*—May Singapore Flourish.

The same words form the title of the national anthem, sung in Malay and written by Zubir Said. Singapore's highest order, the Darjah Utama Temasek, recalls its ancient Malay name.

4   THE PEOPLE

FOUNDED in 1819, Singapore had a population of 52,891 by 1850. A century later, it reached the million mark; and by the middle of 1971 totalled 2,110,400, with a population density of 9,220 persons per square mile. In contrast to the prewar years, when it owed so much to immigration, the population growth is now almost entirely due to the natural rate of increase, which is 17 per 1,000 of population. About 75 per cent of the republic's citizens are Singapore-born, and more than 50 per cent of them are under twenty years of age. The sex ratio, until the 1930s heavily weighted in favour of men, has evened out at about 1,065 males per 1,000 females. An exception is found in the Indian-Pakistani section of the population, where the imbalance in favour of males reflects the continued transience of the immigrants in this group until recent years.

Seventy-six per cent of the population of Singapore are Chinese; less than 15 per cent are Malays; about 7 per cent are Indian or Pakistani by origin. Apart from the *orang laut*, Singapore had no native population in the beginning. Its mixture of peoples is an accident of history, and in the first instance an artificial by-product of British imperialism. In 1824, the first census showed a population of 10,683, of whom 4,850 were Malays, 3,317 Chinese, 1,925 Bugis from Indonesia, 756 Indians, 74 Europeans, 16 Armenians and 15 Arabs.

The Chinese were the earliest plantation owners and from the start prominent in commerce. There were no Malay merchants. Cameron, writing in 1865, describes the Malays as 'literate, but unambitious' and early European settlers appear to have found

74

Period	Total All Races			Malays (1)			Chinese			Indians and Pakistanis (2)			Other Races		
	Persons	M	F	Persons	M	F	Persons	M	F	Persons	M	F	Persons	M	F
1871 Census	97·1	74·3	22·8	26·1	14·6	11·5	54·6	47·1	7·5	11·5	9·5	2·0	4·9	3·1	1·8
1881 Census	137·8	104·1	33·7	33·0	18·5	14·5	86·8	72·6	14·2	12·1	9·7	2·4	5·9	3·3	2·6
1891 Census	181·6	138·4	43·2	36·0	20·9	15·1	121·9	100·4	21·5	16·0	12·9	3·1	7·7	4·2	3·5
1901 Census	227·6	170·0	57·6	36·0	20·2	15·8	164·0	130·4	33·6	17·8	14·3	3·5	9·8	5·1	4·7
1911 Census	303·3	215·5	87·8	41·8	22·6	19·2	219·5	161·6	57·9	27·8	23·1	4·7	14·2	8·2	6·0
1921 Census	418·3	280·9	137·4	53·6	29·6	24·0	315·1	214·2	100·9	32·3	26·9	5·4	17·3	10·2	7·1
1931 Census	557·7	352·1	205·6	65·0	34·9	30·1	418·6	261·0	157·6	50·8	42·8	8·0	23·3	13·4	9·9
1947 Census	938·2	515·0	423·2	113·8	62·3	51·5	729·5	387·4	342·1	69·0	51·7	17·3	25·9	13·6	12·3
1957 Census	1,445·9	762·8	683·1	197·0	103·2	93·8	1,090·6	555·7	534·9	124·1	86·0	38·1	34·2	17·9	16·3
1970 Census	2,074·5	1,062·1	1,012·3	311·3	158·4	152·9	1,579·8	796·4	783·3	145·1	87·5	57·6	38·0	19·7	18·3

POPULATION BY RACIAL GROUP AND SEX

(1) includes Indonesians (2) includes Ceylonese. 'Other Races' includes all persons from other ethnic groups, such as Eurasians, Europeans, Arabs, Japanese, Jews and others.

them the most congenial among the Asian races—perhaps because their very lack of interest in commerce caused them to seem more gentlemanly than either Indians or Chinese. Cameron remarks, as an illustration of the way in which their functions in society were different from those of the Chinese, that he 'had never heard of a Chinese groom or coachman, or of a Malay tailor'. For the Malays from the peninsula and the Bugis, Balinese and Javanese from Indonesia to return to their country of origin was relatively easy, and perhaps there was correspondingly less incentive for them to gain a firm economic place in the new community. In contrast, most of the original Chinese settlers arrived, especially in the last third of the nineteenth century, armed with the energy of desperation. For the most part they came from China itself, leaving a country of unstable government and natural disaster, and a bondage often worse than that of animals, to seek their fortune in Singapore.

The Indians were different again in the circumstances of their arrival. There had been Indian traders in the Malay peninsula and the archipelago at least since the first century AD, but those Indians who settled for any length of time in Singapore after the British settlement came, in the early years, as convicts or as soldiers. The convicts were those sentenced to transportation by the Indian authorities : the first of them arrived in 1825 and Singapore ceased to be an Indian penal colony only in 1873, when convicts were sent instead to the Andaman islands. Upon reaching the end of their sentence, they were compelled to remain in Singapore for an equivalent number of years more, and many of them became honest and hard-working citizens. Most of the public buildings of the colony's first fifty years, and virtually all the roads, were built by their labour. Other Indians originally arrived with the armies of the East India Company, as hewers of wood and drawers of water, cobblers, laundrymen and shopkeepers.

In the last decades of the nineteenth century there was a great influx of Indian labourers who worked on the coffee estates of Malaya; after the turn of the century they migrated to the newly developed rubber plantations. Many settled in Singapore for a number of years, though they intended eventually to return to their families. It is comparatively recently that the Indians have become a stable and substantial part of Singapore's population.

Today, the races remain physically distinct for the most part. But it is religion and national customs, rather than origin, which separate them. All the nationalities substantially represented in the population have their own cultures, rituals and feast days, and, as in the earliest days of the settlement, large groups of one race tend to live in certain areas, though this is gradually being changed by the government's housing board policy.

Among peoples of such widely differing attitudes, some friction is to be expected, and from time to time, as in the religious riots surrounding the Bertha Hertogh case of 1950 and the racial riots between Malays and Chinese in 1964, it has risen to an intensity which breaks out in bloody violence. How the differences affect everyday life in Singapore may be illustrated in its simplest form by the problem of providing food for a multi-racial lunch or dinner party : pork, which is the favourite food of the Chinese, is forbidden to Malays and to Indians of the Muslim faith; beef is forbidden to the Hindus, and meat of all kinds to some Indian groups, and if the guests include Eurasians they are most likely Catholic, forbidden to eat meat on Fridays. Yet in general the races co-exist amicably. They work side by side in the police force and on national service; they sit together in the classrooms of integrated schools.

A recent survey conducted by sociologists from the University of Singapore showed that nine out of ten citizens now prefer to call themselves 'Singaporeans' rather than Chinese, Indian, Malay or whatever other racial identity they may lay claim to.

THE CHINESE

The Chinese, even within China, are by no means a homogeneous people. Though the written language is the same everywhere, the

77

spoken languages of China are many, and the characteristics of the inhabitants of the various provinces are markedly dissimilar.

In the written instructions given by Raffles in 1822, pertaining to the laying-out of the original Chinese quarter, he speaks of the disputes to be expected between those originating in different provinces. Today, the various 'tribes', as the European settlers once spoke of them, remain distinct in language, and to some extent in appearance, customs and means of livelihood.

The main sections of Singapore's Chinese population comprise the Cantonese, the Teochews, the Hokkiens (also known as the Fukienese), the Hainanese or Hylams, the Hakkas, and those from Kwangsi province. The Hokkiens engage largely in trade and shopkeeping, the Cantonese are most often artisans. The Teochews work at manual occupations, mostly in the port and harbour, and the Hainanese in hotels or domestic service. The limits of their various trades are surprisingly well-marked : even in an area as small as that of the Orchard Road covered market, all the butchers are Hainanese and virtually all the sellers of fruit, vegetables and flowers Teochew, with a few Hokkienese keeping ironmongery or grocery stalls.

Some mistrust still exists between the speakers of the various Chinese dialects. Singapore Hokkiens visiting Hong Kong, which is almost entirely populated by Cantonese, speak angrily on their return of the way they were treated as country cousins and looked down on because of the way they pronounce Cantonese.

In the nineteenth century, Chinese immigrants fell naturally into four sections of society : the merchants, the planters, the artisans, and the 'coolies', labourers engaged in rural employment on the estates inland. Today, though the private planters have almost disappeared, along with the plantations, the internal ebb and flow of goods remains largely in the hands of the Chinese; the artisans are still there in Chinatown and have spread out to the suburbs, and farming and vegetable-growing are virtually Chinese monopolies.

Traditionally, Chinese society is based on a cellular system, whereby individual freedom counts for nothing beside family loyalty, and family loyalty is outweighed by the duty owed to the clan. Clan solidarity remains a prominent feature of Chinese life in Singapore, though it is now normally expressed in membership of an association. The clan associations are a form of insurance for their members of the kind provided by friendly societies or freemasonry in Europe : they assist members in financial distress or need of legal aid, help widows and orphans, and add prestige and help with expenses on occasions such as weddings or funerals.

The ritual most frequently observed in the open street is that of the funeral cortège. The coffin is usually placed on a lorry, decorated in garish colours with a painted canopy, surmounted by a stork, if the corpse is a woman's, and by a dragon-like lion if it is a man's. The mourners, who may precede the coffin perched in the back of another lorry, wear roughly made hoods of unbleached calico. Clan members or professional mourners, dressed in white and wearing the insignia of the association, may walk before the coffin, beating drums and clanging cymbals to frighten the evil spirits thought to lie along the route. Often the procession takes a roundabout way to the cemetery, to allow persons in the surrounding district to pay their respects, and the lorry bearing the coffin frequently has tow ropes attached to the bonnet so that the procession may pause for a symbolic 'pulling of the coffin'. Association members leave the cemetery before the actual burial. Red is the lucky Chinese colour, and the coffin will have a piece of red paper caught in the lid, to keep away evil spirits. Paper lanterns hanging from staffs are stuck into the filled-in grave. A photograph of the deceased is fixed on the headstone, which ideally is situated in a favourable position determined by a geomancer.

The services of geomancers, together with those of Taoist and Buddhist priests, undertakers and professional mourners, are concentrated at the 'death-houses' which the Chinese support throughout Malaya wherever there is a sufficiency of their own people. The death-houses, which in Singapore may soon be driven by urban renewal from their famous haunts in Sago Lane, were, until recent years, lodgings where those who believed themselves near to death awaited their time, though they were sometimes also used by people not mortally ill but too sick to be looked after in the *kongsis*, communal lodging-rooms. Now, the death-houses, though still extremely picturesque to a western eye in some of the services they provide, are little more than a local variations on funeral parlours.

The elaborate garments and heavy jewels formerly worn by bridal couples are no longer in use. Most Chinese brides wear white dresses and veils in western style. The custom of *yam sing*, however, is still followed. By this, the bride and groom must go from table to table at the wedding reception, toasting their guests; traditionally, the glass must be drained at each cry of *yam sing*.

Only about 3 per cent of the Singapore Chinese are Christians, and most of these are Methodists, since this was the sect particularly active in Malaya during early missionary days. In traditional Chinese religion, three strains are to be distinguished : Taoism, Confucianism, and Buddhism. In general, the Chinese combine elements of all three, together with a number of superstitions and beliefs in magical practices.

Taoism provides most of the extensive mythology and numerous deities of the Chinese; Buddhism is represented in a much debased form. Some idea of the extraordinary result of the mixture may be gained from a visit to Haw Par Villa, also known as the Tiger Balm Gardens, at Pasir Panjang, which is open free of charge. Here, over several acres, the legends and deities of the Chinese and all the tortures of the Buddhist hell are represented in gaudily painted concrete.

Confucianism is represented mainly by ancestor worship, and a majority of Chinese homes and many places of business maintain an 'ancestor shelf' on the wall, at which joss sticks are burned and food is offered. There is usually a representation of the kitchen god nearby, to which offerings are also made. For many of the younger generation, all this is a matter of routine cultural acknowledgement rather than deep personal belief.

Feasts and Festivals

The Singapore year provides a great variety of festivals, because of the multi-racial character of the population, and among them at least six of the eight major traditional Chinese celebrations continue to be widely observed. Before Chinese New Year, almost all Chinese, whatever their religious beliefs, try to pay debts and make up quarrels. On New Year's Eve, most of them organise dinners at which the family in all its extensions is present; on the first days of the New Year, freshly barbered and dressed in new clothes, they pay numerous visits to relatives and worship their ancestors and the gods. At midnight on New Year's Eve, strings of crimson firecrackers were traditionally set alight, their deafening reports supposedly frightening away evil spirits and welcoming the kitchen god on his return from heaven, where he had been reporting on the family's activities over the year. Few customs are so firmly rooted as the setting-off of crackers, and thousands of pounds' worth used to be exploded in Singapore during the year, particularly at Chap Goh Meh (formerly called the Feast of Lanterns), which marks the end of the New Year celebrations. Recently, however, the firing of crackers has been placed under restrictions, owing to the loss of life and property in fires and explosions.

Children at New Year are presented with *ang pow*, gifts of money wrapped in tiny packets; the customary New Year greeting is *'Kung hey fatt choy!'*—a wish for good fortune and prosperity. Each year is named after one of the animals in the Chinese zodiac, so that the year of the rat follows that of the pig, the pig that of the dog, and so on, each year being supposed to show certain characteristics of the animal in question (the others include chicken, monkey, goat, horse, snake, dragon, hare, tiger and ox). Some years are therefore considered luckier than others, according to the nature of the undertaking proposed.

At the festival of Ching Ming, the family graves are swept and tended, red candles are lighted upon them, and offerings of food and drink are made. At the Feast of the Seven Sisters, young girls pray for husbands. Seven or eight days later comes the Feast of Hungry Ghosts. According to traditional beliefs, on this one day of the year the gates of hell are opened, and neglected spirits who have no one to sacrifice to them come out in search of food. It is at this time that mediums in the temples claim to communicate with spirits of the dead on behalf of relatives.

The observances of the Dragon Boat festival are not so obvious to the foreigner, since no dragon boat races are held in Singapore, but some of the Chinese eat special rice dumplings, worship the family gods, and chase away evil spirits with red paper charms.

The important mid-autumn festival is a time for eating mooncakes with various rich fillings. The celebrations are in honour of the moon goddess and the hare who makes the drug of immortality on the moon. This is particularly a festival for women and children. Chinese shops blossom into bunches of brightly coloured cellophane lanterns, made to represent all manner of things, from dragons to space ships. Enchanting processions of children, their lighted lanterns bobbing, thread their way along dark lanes by night.

The Double Ninth festival is not much followed, except for Taoist pilgrimages to the island of Kusu. The eighth traditional festival, the Winter Solstice, is also not made much of in Singapore, except with prayers to the family gods.

There is no doubt that the hold of the various festivals, most of which have no genuine religious content, is weakening on the educated Chinese, but the majority continue to observe them in some degree, and often claim that a substantial win in a lottery, for example, is a direct result of having worshipped one's ancestors at the appropriate times.

There are a number of larger Chinese temples in Singapore,

where the respectful foreign visitor is welcome. The Tean Hock Kiong temple in Telok Ayer Street was completed in 1842, and is dedicated to the Hokkien sea goddess Ma-Cho-Po. There are other notable temples in Kim Keat Avenue and Race Course Road, and hundreds of smaller ones scattered about the city. In them are to be found the last vestiges of traditional Chinese architecture in Singapore : cylindrical rooftiles, scarlet lacquered posts, dipping eaves and tiered pagodas, and above all the glazed porcelain dragons.

Little has survived of traditional Chinese costume in the everyday life of Singapore. Even the shortened version of the *cheongsam*, the dress with side-slits and high collar, is not much favoured by young girls, though older women commonly wear it. More often to be seen is the *samfoo*, the costume of trousers and high-collared tunic worn usually by women of the poorer classes. The nearest everyday approaches to traditional costume are the mid-blue *samfoo* and blood-red, square-topped head-dress of the Samsui labouring women; the huge conical woven hats of Cantonese women foodhawkers; and the black wide-legged trousers, white tunics and pulled-back hair of the more elderly *amahs*, the domestic servants. Most young Chinese women wear the latest western fashions.

THE MALAYS

The ancestors of the Malay peoples of the archipelago probably came from southern China between 2,500 and 1,500 BC. Since then, there has been a great deal of intermarriage with the other peoples of South East Asia, but the Malays of Singapore are fairly easily distinguishable from the other inhabitants. They are a graceful people, usually of medium height, with brown skins and black hair, which among the women is often luxuriantly wavy. Temperamentally, they are very different from the Chinese, and even today show little interest in commerce or in money-making for its own sake, preferring to make a ready response to the simple pleasures of life. Many Malays are extremely hard workers, but for them work is only a part of life; whereas for many Chinese it is, aside from their families, everything.

Although they have been privileged since 1969 to have free education up to university level if their parents are Singapore citizens, only 2·1 per cent of the total enrolment of the 1970–1 session of the University of Singapore was made up by Malays, and at the same date they represented only about 2 per cent of those in administrative, executive and managerial positions, and only 5·9 per cent of those in the professional, technical and related classes. It is not, however, clear whether they simply do not value the kind of advancement on which Westerners and Chinese set such store, or whether they fail to seek it out of poverty or ignorance. Traditional Malay life is fast disappearing along with the *kampong*, and the question of what place the Malays will assume in the community is a pressing and a potentially dangerous one, surrounded as Singapore is by Malay powers.

Islam became firmly established in South East Asia after the conversion of the ruler of Malacca, in the early fifteenth century, and virtually all Malays are Muslims. The 'five pillars of faith' for the Muslim are prayer, fasting, almsgiving, pilgrimage, and belief in Allah and his apostle Mohammed. Pork and wine are forbidden, and Friday is the sacred day, when the men meet in the mosque at noon for prayer, the women normally praying at home.

Fasting between the hours of sunrise and sunset is enjoined on all Muslims except the sick, young children and travellers during Ramadan, the ninth month of the Muslim calendar. At the end of this period comes the feast of Hari Raya Puasa when the Malays virtually keep open house; relatives pay visits, and even the poorest attempt to obtain new shoes, if not a full suit of clothes to wear. Malay wives clean the house from top to bottom, and hang new curtains. Special prayers are offered, and the strict Muslim makes peace with all his enemies.

Another time of celebration is Hari Raya Haji, which marks

the conclusion of the annual pilgrimage to Mecca. Other days which are of special significance to the Muslim population include the birthday of Mohammed; Mandi Safar, commemorating the end of a month-long illness suffered by the prophet; and Nisfu, at which the dead are especially remembered and filial visits take place.

Underlying adherence to the tenets of Islam proper, there remain many ancient superstitions, and there is a widespread belief among the uneducated in magic worked by *jinn*, spirits of good or of evil.

The Malays cling to their national dress to a considerable extent, and, whilst perhaps a majority of the women wear it daily, at times of festival many of the men also dress traditionally. The Malay male costume consists of a loose collarless jacket, the *baju*, worn over loose trousers. A *kain*, a cloth with decorated border, is tied round the waist over the jacket, reaching the knee. The *songkok*, a black velvet cap with stiffened sides, is often worn by men and boys, even on ordinary days. The white skullcap denotes the *haji*, who has made the pilgrimage to Mecca.

Batik, which is a method of patterning cloth by first drawing on it in wax and then dyeing it, originated in Java and is particularly associated with the Malays of the archipelago. The *batik* patterns are nowadays imitated by industrial machinery, and it is mostly this cheaper cloth which is worn by the Malays of Singapore. Malay women, at least those of the *kampong*, wear a full-length *kain* of *batik* cotton cloth, and a longsleeved loose tunic, the *baju kurong*, or a close-fitting jacket, the *kebaya*. Whereas the smart Chinese woman's slender figure and style of dress make her appear all angles, the elegant Malay woman is all curves: partly as a matter of natural endowment, partly from the use of a tight waist-corset worn beneath the *kebaya*. The *baju kurong*, as concealing as the *kebaya* is revealing, is often worn as a uniform by Malay schoolgirls.

Extravagant versions of the elaborate Malay bridal costumes, which derive from those of ancient Hindu princes and princesses,

F

are to be seen at the various representations of the *bersanding* performed at certain hotels in Singapore as a tourist entertainment. The *bersanding*, though often misleadingly referred to as a Malay wedding, is in fact the ceremony in which the bridegroom, having left the house of the bride's parents after the marriage, returns to claim her. The bride is not present at the actual marriage, which is normally performed by the groom repeating a prescribed form of words whilst facing the *kathi*, or local registrar, and signing the register of Muslim marriages.

Funeral customs are simpler than those of the Chinese. A Muslim is usually buried within a few hours of death, and the 'coffin' is a stretcher with an arched wooden lid. The body is placed in a recess in one wall of the grave, lying in its right side and facing Mecca, with the wooden cover over it. The grave has a stone marker.

Singapore's first mosque, known as the Malacca mosque, was built in 1820 in Omar Road. The largest mosque, the Sultan mosque, was completed in 1928, though there was an earlier building on the site in the 1820s.

THE INDIANS

A large part of the textile trade of the republic is in Indian hands, and the Nattukottai *chettiars*, a caste of southern Indians from the district of Madras, have long been established as moneylenders and bankers. Punjabis and Sikhs work mainly in urban occupations, as clerks in commercial or financial concerns, or in government service. Many Sikhs work as policemen, taxidrivers, and —their traditional occupation—*jagas*, or watchmen.

Roughly 70 per cent of Singapore's population of Indian origin are Hindu, 20 per cent Muslim, 5 per cent Christian, and 2 per cent Sikh, and there are some Parsees. Generally speaking, Muslims and Hindus are on civil terms, but there is little social mixing.

There is some intermarriage between Indians of the Muslim

faith and Malays, though usually the former belong to the Hanafi sect, and the latter to the Shafi'i, which has tenets less favourable to the freedom of women.

The Indians and Pakistanis of Singapore, unlike the Chinese and the Malays, still have a noticeably uneven sex ratio as a result of their traditional pattern of immigration. Hindu emphasis on purity and pollution, questions of caste, and the feeling of many Hindus that Hinduism is not, essentially, a matter of conviction, but something one is born to, have stood in the way of inter-marriage.

The two great Hindu festivals in Singapore are Thaipusam and Deepavali. At Thaipusam the image of Subrahmanya, one of the minor deities, and the eldest son of Shiva the Destroyer (the other supreme deities are Brahma the Creator and Vishnu the Preserver) is taken in procession round the streets at the end of the day. Earlier, devotees parade, performing acts of self-mortification, their skins pierced with needles, their faces penetrated by silver arrows. Some carry *kavadis*, spiked structures resting on the penitent's shoulders and forming a semicircle over his head. Even children sometimes bear a *kavadi*, usually to fulfil a vow made by their parents in thanksgiving for their return to health.

Deepavali, the festival of lights, commemorates the victory of Lord Krishna, the ninth incarnation of Vishnu, over the demon king Narakasura. It is a gay occasion, and gifts of flowers and fruits are taken to the temple, whilst there are special celebrations in the home.

In the second week of October, a fire-walking ceremony is usually held at the Mariamman temple in South Bridge Road, which, like the *chettiar* temple in Tank Road, was built in the nineteenth century by the Indian convict labour force. Barefoot devotees walk across a pit which is three feet deep and filled with burning wood and incense.

Hinduism has many deities, and images of them decorate the walls and roofs of temples with their painted brilliance and great variety of human and semi-animal figures. The more recently built temples, like the one in Orchard Road, are faced with glazed tiling. Hinduism shares with Buddhism a belief in reincarnation. Hindus are cremated at death.

Hindu marriages are normally arranged by the parents, though in most cases today with the consent of the bride and groom, who may, however, have met only once before the ceremony, and then only in the company of others. The bride brings a dowry, and the ceremony is usually performed in the home. The most vital part of the ritual is for the bride and groom to take seven symbolic steps round the sacred fire together.

The Sikhs are the most instantly identifiable of Singapore's racial and religious groups, because of the ban which their religion traditionally imposes on the cutting of hair and beard. Their turbans, or, in the case of young boys, their topknots bound with cloth, and the steel bangles they must wear, mark them out. Some of the younger Sikhs now cut their hair and leave off the turban. Their religion is a combination of elements from Hinduism and Islam.

The Parsees, who have been established in Singapore as merchants since the 1880s, are followers of an ancient religion of the Persian Zoroaster, and monotheists.

Vesak Day, the Buddhist celebration which falls in May, is a public holiday in Singapore, though Buddhism in its pure form is observed only by the Sinhalese section of the community, and by some of South Indian, Burmese and Thai extraction.

THE EURASIANS

Singapore Eurasians number about 20,000, and a great many of them are descended from the Portuguese communities of Malacca, Macao, and Goa. Consequently many of them are Catholics bearing names such as Albuquerque, D'Cotta, de Silva, de Souza, Lopez, Monteiro, Vas, Xavier, and a host of others. Some still speak the *patois* known as *Cristão* : twelve or thirteen such families were already resident in Singapore by the 1820s.

The Portuguese Mission was very active in Singapore from the early nineteenth century and in 1853 completed St Joseph's Church. St Anthony's Boys' School and the sister school for girls were founded in the 1880s. In the last few decades of the nineteenth century the Eurasian community gathered at a large tract of land, known as 'Tipurarry', off the Changi Road, for celebrations during public and school holidays. Later, the suburb of Katong became their favourite place of residence.

Many Eurasian families have played a prominent part in Singapore, notably the Velges, Reutens, Deskers and the Leicesters, and some are of Dutch or German rather than Portuguese descent. In many ways they had most to gain from the coming of independence : under colonial rule they were unable to obtain the same salary for doing the same work as Europeans, who might be dismissed from their work if they associated with them. A silent witness to their situation was the Eurasian recreation club on the west side of the Padang, facing the European cricket club on the east. An invisible but insurmountable wall divided the territory between them. Today the president himself is a Eurasian; and, in common with people of Sino-Indian or Sino-Malay parentage and other racial mixtures, the Eurasians have an equal place in the community

OTHER NATIONALITIES

There are three synagogues in Singapore, and a Jewish community centring mainly round Bencoolen Street has flourished since the early years of the settlement. Arabs have been prominent in Singapore life since its earliest days; most of those permanently resident are the descendants of nineteenth-century settlers from the Hadramaut. The Armenian community, once sufficiently strong to have its own cathedral, now numbers about thirty. The census of 1871 showed one Japanese in residence; by 1911, there were 1,409, and Braddell writes of a 'gay little Japanese quarter' in the Middle Road area of the 1930s. The present day Japanese population of two or three hundred are mostly businessmen and diplomats.

At the 1957 census the population included 3,471 Arabs, 786 Nepalese Gurkhas (all of them likely to leave Singapore with the disbanding of the Gurkha regiments), 729 Jews, 663 Filippinos, 297 Thais, 194 Japanese, and 136 Burmese.

LANGUAGE

The national language of Singapore is, officially, Malay; but Mandarin Chinese, Tamil (the chief language of South India) and English are all recognised official languages.

The Chinese dialects include Hokkien, Cantonese, Teochew, Hainanese, Hakka and Foochew, and the communities using the first three of these are each more numerous than the whole of the Malay ethnic group. Among the Indian section of the population, Telugu, Malayalam, Punjabi, Hindi and Bengali are spoken.

The English language is arguably the greatest of the legacies left by colonial rule : paradoxically, though it is the native tongue of very few Singapore citizens, it may yet prove the strongest force for national integration, and it is significant that from 1971 it was officially adopted as the main medium used by the Singapore armed forces. Throughout Singapore's history English has been the language of government, and increasingly it has become the language of science and modernisation, through which the mass media of the western world communicate.

Singapore desperately needs modernisation and technological advance within its own industries; it must encourage the investment of foreign capital and all possible commercial development, if it is to survive; and it aims to attract an ever larger number of foreign tourists. For all these reasons, a high percentage of population fluent in English is vital to its future.

Many of the Chinese realise this, although some are reluctant for cultural reasons to concede it. Chinese schools are losing their popularity relative to the other language streams, and their enrolment is declining. The reason is that students who, speaking Chinese at home, learn English only as a second language at school have few conversational opportunities, and leave unable to speak it with any fluency or accuracy. They find themselves at a great disadvantage when seeking work in commerce, trade, or at higher government levels.

The language pattern among the Chinese educated classes is constantly changing. Already, a common situation in the Chinese middle class is that, where the parents of children of school age speak English with their children and Chinese with the grandparents, the children themselves speak Chinese, if at all, only with difficulty. Many Chinese educated in English schools neither speak nor write Chinese.

The English language in some ways papers over the cracks between the races, as it does between the generations. The multi-racial character of the population makes the use of a 'neutral' language an asset : within the context of an independent Singapore, English is no one's language, and therefore it may the more easily become everyone's. The other side of the coin is that the government must tread delicately in encouraging the use of English. It will not do to risk offending not only the Malay and Indian minorities but that large section of the Chinese population which is convinced of the cultural superiority of things Chinese. Moreover, the importance of Mandarin and of Malay is likely to increase in the light of present political developments : another reason why a truly bi-lingual and if possible tri-lingual society is desirable.

Some public signs in Singapore are written in Tamil, which has its own script, and in Malay, though the Jawi script of the Malay is seen only in Malay schools; many such notices are written in the appropriate Chinese ideographs, but all of them are written in English.

SPORTS AND PASTIMES

The first club formed in Singapore was the billiards club, established on 1 October 1829, but it lasted barely a year. The New Year sports, started in 1834, were a much more energetic and successful form of recreation. Originally they were organised by the Europeans as an entertainment for the rest of the population, and for some years mainly took the form of a regatta. The five European-owned boats which took part in the third race on 1 January 1834 constituted the first Singapore yacht club. From 1836 the regatta took place annually in an almost unbroken sequence until the Japanese occupation in 1942. As time went on, pony races, foot races and such entertainments as climbing the greasy pole were added, and public-minded citizens offered prizes and silver cups.

The younger men of the community would leave their offices in Commercial Square (Raffles Place) when the day's work was over to play cricket or fives near the seafront until it grew dark. The Singapore Cricket Club played its first recorded match on the Esplanade on 14 October 1852 and is still a popular centre of social and sporting life.

The first horse races in Singapore were held in February 1843, when the redoubtable W. H. Read won the first Singapore Cup. The first race course is commemorated in the name of Race Course Road; gentleman riders only were allowed to compete for the first quarter of a century. The first record of interest among the Chinese occurs in 1861, when Tan Kim Seng gave a magnificent ball to celebrate race week. Today, the Singapore Turf Club flourishes at Bukit Timah Road and provides one outlet for the traditional Chinese passion for gambling. It holds seven professional and two amateur meetings yearly, and the Chinese in particular are proud horse-owners. Total attendance in 1970 was 389,888; stakes paid amounted to $2,041,300 (£275,400; US $680,100); and turnover on the totalisator was $75,761,910 (£10,238,000; US $25,253,970).

Tennis has been played from 1875, and in 1885 the Straits Chinese Recreation Club was founded for the pursuit of cricket, football and hockey, though by 1883, Song Ong Siang tells us, its activities were confined to tennis, football, chess and billiards. Association football came in 1889, to be followed by rugby, and the Straits Chinese Football Association was formed in 1911. Cricket and association football have in the past drawn some of their best league sides from the British military, who also dominated the throwing events at the meets of the Singapore Athletic Association, and their departure may lead to a slightly different emphasis in Singapore sporting activities. Before the British withdrawal, for example, the Singapore Yacht Association had about 1,000 active members, but five-sixths of its affiliated clubs were British forces' organisations, and most of the boats used were military property. On the other hand, with Singapore's growing prosperity and the splendid facilities it offers, it seems unlikely that yachting will ever cease to be popular. Water-skiing has many adherents, who practise off the coast of Ponggol and Pasir Ris, and skin-diving is popular. There are good angling grounds off the Horsbrugh Lighthouse and in several other places, where snappers, Spanish mackerel, groupers and even sharks are caught.

Some relatively expensive sports have a long history in Singapore. The Singapore Polo Club, founded in 1899, survives. Polo was first played in 1886, and two of its most ardent exponents were Sir Frank Swettenham, Governor of the Straits Settlements from 1901 to 1904, and Sultan Abu Bakar of Johore.

The golf club was founded in 1891. It is recorded that Mr Justice Goldney, the founder, drove the first ball on a nine-hole circuit at the old race course wearing knickerbockers, a stiff collar, white tie, red coat, and bowler hat, and thus inaugurated what has become one of Singapore's most popular sports.

The club moved to Bukit Timah in 1924, where some 275 acres of jungle were cleared to make the course. A second club was formed with a course nearby in 1927, and in 1963 the two merged. The Island Country Club, as it is now known, controls four eighteen-hole courses, on the best of which, the Bukit, the World Golf Cup was played in 1969. The courses are magnificently sited, near the reservoirs of the catchment areas. There are also four nine-hole courses in Singapore, plus a seven-hole course at Tanglin.

The auto club, founded in 1907, became the Singapore Motor Club, which in turn gave way to the combined efforts of the Automobile Association and the Singapore Motor Sports Club. The AA has the franchise of the Fédération Internationale de l'Automobile, and has delegated it to the Motor Sports Club for the purposes of organising the Singapore Grand Prix. This, instituted in the early 1960s, annually attracts motorists of world class, though as yet there is no permanent motor-racing circuit, and the Grand Prix is run on a stretch of road.

Interest in sport was initially a legacy of the British, but it has been strongly encouraged by the PAP government, which has been quick to see that, apart from its contribution to health, participation in team sports and entry in international competitions is one of the surest ways to build a sense of nationhood. Sport takes a prominent position in school activities, and it is compulsory for every able-bodied child in government schools to participate in some form. Athletic activities begun in school continue, for boys at least, during national service. Physical toughness is especially inculcated at the Outward Bound School, established in 1968 on Pulau Ubin, where about a dozen courses are annually held. Because of its importance in bringing the various races together, sport enjoys some priority in the national budget. There are four public swimming pools in addition to several private clubs, and a child can swim for three hours for less than the price of a soft drink, thanks to government subsidies. All the new Housing Development Board estates will have their own sports complexes, including tracks and swimming pools, and the first of these have already been built at Queenstown and Toa Payoh.

In 1966 the first *Pesta Sukan,* the festival of sport, took place, and now accompanies the National Day celebrations held in August. In 1971 participants from twenty countries competed in archery, athletics, basketball, cricket, cycling, women's football, hockey, netball, polo, rugby, soccer, shooting, softball, tenpin bowling and wrestling, in addition to the traditional Malay sport of *sepak takraw,* a game with a rattan ball in which the use of arms and hands is forbidden. All these sports boast their own club or association in Singapore, and other popular activities are badminton, fencing, lawn tennis, swimming, volleyball and weightlifting.

The International Sports Complex, to be completed in 1972, has been built on the site of the old Kallang Airport runway. It will include an indoor area to cater for gymnastics, table tennis, basketball, volleyball, badminton and *sepak takraw*; national stadium facilities for athletics, football, rugby, hockey, rallies, tattoos and concerts, which will give room for 50,000 spectators and the possibility of expanding to accommodate 100,000; living accommodation for visiting teams, and offices for the National Sports Promotion Board, which organises sporting events and controls the thirty-eight sports bodies in the republic. Private facilities such as an ice-skating rink will be added, and there will be two smaller stadiums, seating 6,000 and 9,000 spectators respectively.

As in other important respects, Singapore's small size and multi-racial composition are both a help and a hindrance in achieving success. With so small a population, it is unlikely to achieve a large number of outstanding results in future Asian Games or South East Asian Peninsula Games. At the same time, its people have a wide variety of physique and traditional athletic skills, though this in its turn tends to dissipate effort in particular sports, since so large a number is available. There are, for example, many different forms of pugilism, and there is not only an amateur boxing association, but also a judo association, a wrestling association, and clubs for the pursuit of karate and the Korean art of *tae-kwan-do*. The *Pesta Sukan* holds two chess tournaments : one in international chess and the other in Chinese chess.

There is little doubt that sport for pleasure has a tremendous future in Singapore. Not only is it possible to play games all the year round, thanks to the climate, but new forms of sport continue to blossom. Thus, the fairly recent establishment of public bowling alleys, of a sub-aqua club and an annual race-walking contest which attracts hundred of competitors, have now been followed by the setting up of a parachuting club. The government has established a junior flying club, which trains a limited number of boys and girls for a private pilot's licence at nominal cost. The Singapore Flying Club itself dates from 1927, and is still active.

Traditional forms of entertainment and exercise still have their place : groups of students engage in the graceful, ghostly movements of Chinese shadow-boxing, and although the *wayang*, or popular Chinese opera, has shown some decline recently, temporary stages are still erected for its performance at times of festival. The Malay dance, the *ronggeng*, which originated in the royal courts, is now seen mainly in its modern form, the *joget moden*, danced to western pop music.

So far cultural activities lag behind sport in capturing the interest of Singaporeans, perhaps because the society is not yet settled enough to produce a native literature, art or music of high quality. There are one or two good local painters, including Thomas Yeo and Seah Kim Joo, who has developed the application to painting of the waxing and dyeing methods used in designing *batik* cloth. (The first to do this was Chua Thean Teng). The art museum of the University of Singapore, founded in 1953, has a fine collection of South East Asian art in many forms, and there is a section devoted to the work of modern local artists.

Singapore enjoys the services of what is both the national library and the main public library. It has three branches, at Queenstown, Joo Chiat and Siglap, with a fourth soon to be added at Toa Payoh, and twelve mobile libraries which visit outlying districts. Books in languages other than English were first added in 1956, and the collection now includes fiction and non-fiction in all four official languages. Special collections include music scores and books in braille. The ordinance making it a free public and national library was enacted in 1957; previously it was a subscription library dating back to 1844 and originating as part of Raffles' plan for an educational institution. Its history is closely connected with that of the national museum, which maintains a reference library of more than 120,000 bound volumes of scientific periodicals and books. Two scientific journals are published periodically. These are the *Bulletin of the National Museum*, which covers geology, and the *Memoirs of the National Museum*, covering history and ethnology.

It remains to be seen how far the British withdrawal, which led to the closure of some established drama clubs, will affect the amateur stage, though there are several devoted amateur drama producers among Singapore citizens. The tradition is a long one : amateur theatricals were a favourite form of amusement from 1833 onwards.

In 1960 the National Theatre Trust was founded; the National Theatre was completed in 1963, but it was not until 1968 that the National Theatre Company was established as a centre for amateur dance, music and drama. The company, initially quasi-professional, is intended to become ultimately fully so, but from time to time has run into financial difficulties, and it is uncertain how great a part it will eventually play in Singapore life. In contrast, there are seventy-two cinemas, showing features in all four languages.

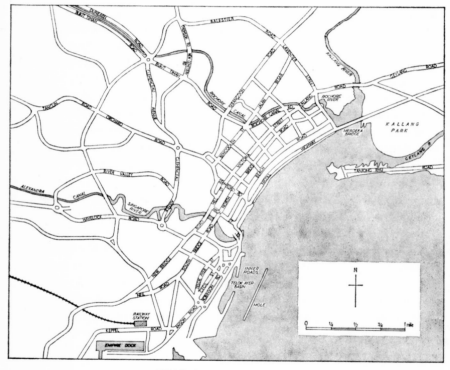

SINGAPORE: CITY AREA

5   COMMUNICATIONS

WHEN Raffles fixed on Singapore as the place for a British settlement, he chose one of the great natural crossroads of the world. The position to which it grew as the hub of the Britain-India-China trade, and as the collection and distribution centre for the islands of South East Asia, was all that he had looked for. Later events, such as the growing importance of Australasia, the use of the telegraph, the building of road and rail networks on the Asian mainland, and, more recently, the development of civil aviation, served to give it yet greater advantages. Today it lies at the centre of a web of worldwide communications, north from the Asian mainland, south from Australasia and Indonesia, west from Europe, Africa and India, and east from America and Japan, China and the Philippines, a web on which its growing industrial economy is dependent.

BOATS AND SHIPS

In January 1819, when Raffles landed from one of a squadron of East India Company ships, he may have seen a few of the white-sailed Malay boats, *kolehs*, sailing what is now the fourth busiest harbour in the world. There was nothing else. By 9 April of the same year, there were two merchantmen and more than 100 small Asian vessels in the harbour. Some of the native craft may be seen virtually unchanged at Boat Quay or in the Inner Roads today. They included sampans, junks, ladder-masted Bugis ships, the shallow-draft seagoing barge known as a *tongkang*, and the Malay *prahu*, which, though widely used for trade, became

99

notorious as the ship of piracy during most of the nineteenth century.

The first China trade ship, the *Earl Balcarres*, arrived on 10 June 1821. In the first $2\frac{1}{2}$ years of the settlement, 2,889 vessels entered and cleared the port, 383 of them being owned and commanded by Europeans, and 2,506 by non-Europeans. Their united tonnage amounted to 161,000 tons. By 1835 the combined annual tonnage was 194,039 tons, and 517 square-rigged ships and 37,521 native vessels entered and cleared the port. The keel of the first seagoing vessel built in Singapore was laid by William Temperton in a boatyard on the north bank of Boat Quay in 1829; she was the brig *Elizabeth*, 194 tons. Sailing ships continued to anchor in the roads for many decades, and included opium clippers from Bombay, which began to reach Canton sailing against the northeast monsoon in the 1830s. Cameron describes the 'network of spars and rigging' which characterised the harbour in the early 1860s, and notes that 'the box-shaped, heavy-rigged East Indiamen that thirty years ago carried the then moderate freight of the island have been exchanged for the beautifully modelled clipper or frigate-built ships'. In Cameron's day, there were never fewer than 500 small craft to be seen in the first reach of the Singapore river, and the Chinese with their shoeboats and the Malays with their sampans catered for passengers and luggage, whilst the Klings (South Indians) managed the *tongkangs*.

Sail and steam worked together when HM sloop *Wolf*, which was sent to Singapore in 1836 to hunt down pirate *prahus*, was joined a year later by the steamship *Diana*. The first steamship ever to call at Singapore was the Dutch *Van Der Capellan*, on 17 April 1827, but it was 1843 before the Straits Settlements were linked by steam, initially by the SS *Victoria*, and 1845 when the first mail steamer, the *Lady Mary Wood*, arrived, as part of the P & O monthly service to China via Ceylon, Singapore and Hong Kong. A regular monthly steamship service between Calcutta and the Straits Settlements was inaugurated in 1846. In September 1848, the first Singapore-built steamer was launched by

Page 101 (above) Lower middle-class Straits Chinese family at the turn of the century. The woman and her daughter wear *nyonya* costume; the man and boy Chinese dress with Western headgear; *(right)* traditional Straits Chinese wedding, Singapore 1959. Such costly weddings are now very rare, but umbrellas are still sometimes used to protect the couple from evil spirits

Page 102 (above) The multi-racial society: school sports day, 1971; *(below)* the National Theatre: begun in celebration of self-government in 1959, it was completed in 1963. Its open-sided auditorium seats 3,420 at performances of ballet, pop music, and orchestral concerts

Wilkinson, Tivendale and Company. She was the *Ranee*, 60ft long, 8ft 6in beam, mechanically powered, and intended for anti-piracy duties off the Borneo coast. In 1852, the 700 ton *Chusan*, the first vessel on the new P & O Singapore–Australia run, arrived from Australia, and Singapore then became an ocean junction. By the early 1860s, says Cameron, there were always six to twelve steamers in port, some of them men-of-war. A sensation was caused during the American Civil War by the appearance in port of the Confederate cruiser *Alabama*, which had recently destroyed three American ships near the Sunda Straits.

The opening of the Suez Canal in 1869 was a death blow to the great tea clippers which called at Singapore on the way to Australia, as they were unable to use the short cut. Their approaching demise was signalled by the setting aside, in 1871, of new berthage at the wharves for the coaling of China tea steamers. New docks, built in the 1860s, took into account the depth of the Suez Canal, since most oceangoing vessels were now constructed with a view to its requirements. With the change to steam and the opening of Suez, tonnage entering and clearing the port annually rose from 200,000 tons in 1869 to over 700,000 in 1872. The average tonnage of square-rigged vessels entering the port rose from 626 tons in 1870 to nearly 2,000 tons registered in 1905. Rudyard Kipling, visiting Singapore in 1889, noted 'five solid miles of masts and funnels along the water front'.

Some of the ships of the 1880s and the men who sailed them are to be found thinly disguised in the novels of Joseph Conrad, who was several times at Singapore. The fate of the pilgrim ship *Patna* which brought Lord Jim in the novel of that name to his moment of truth is based on that of the steamship *Jeddah*, Singapore-owned, which left port in July 1880 with 953 pilgrims bound for Jeddah, and was abandoned by the European crew when it sprang a leak. The subsequent action for salvage, held at Singapore, caused the scandal to be widely known.

Today, ships of fifty countries and 200 shipping lines converge on Singapore. Coastal vessels and harbour craft, of which there are 2,500, used for lighterage, passenger transport and food supply to ships, anchor in the Inner Roads, and seagoing lighters trade with nearby islands and Malaysia. The larger fishing vessels anchor at South Pier, and government launches lie at the Master Attendant's Pier. Large oceangoing vessels anchor in the Outer Roads beyond the breakwater. Giant tankers of 200,000dwt tons and over anchored at the conventional buoy mooring system off Pulau Bukom for the first time in 1971.

The government established its own register of Singapore ships on 2 September 1966, and in 1968 'flag of convenience' laws were enacted permitting the tax-free registration of ships owned in other countries. The national shipping line, Neptune Orient Lines Ltd, which was incorporated on 30 December 1968, operates a regular liner service of worldwide range, and has tankers and freighters for charter.

Lighthouses

In the early days of the British settlement, a light to guide ships was fixed to the flagstaff of the signal station on the island of Blakang Mati. The signal station was moved to Mount Faber in 1845, and another was later erected on Fort Canning. In 1902 the Fort Canning Lighthouse, an all-steel hollow structure, about 80ft high but 202ft above sea level, was lit by a 75mm burner with 20,000 candlepower, which gave it visibility for about 18 nautical miles. By 1958 it had outlived its usefulness, since its light was now obscured by the skyscrapers of the waterfront, and its function was taken over by a new revolving electric beacon in the centre of the roof of Fullerton Building.

The port of Singapore continues to have its main signal station on Mount Faber, with subsidiaries at Tanjong Belayar and Jurong as well as at Fullerton Building. Of the five lighthouses, the Horsbrugh, built in 1850 on the island of Pedra Branca, at the eastern entrance to the Singapore Straits, and Pulau Pisang, built in 1902 43 miles to the west of Singapore, are outside port limits. The others are Sultan Shoal, Raffles (built on Pulau

Sakumu in 1854 to mark the western entrance to the Singapore Straits), and Fullerton. In addition the port has 65 beacons, 38 of them fitted with lights, and 27 buoys, 18 of them fitted with lights.

OVERLAND TRAVEL

Coming to Singapore for the second time on 31 May 1819, Raffles brought with him bullocks for the use of the officer in charge of public works, and bullock carts continued in use at least until World War II. Other early forms of transport included sedan chairs and *redis*, introduced by the Chinese, ponies imported from Acheh, and various types of horse-drawn carriage, including 'palankeen carriages' made on the island. The *redi*, used by well-to-do Chinese women, was a hammock slung on poles, with a thick palm-leaf cover, in which were peepholes, thrown over it. In the 1840s and 1850s, buggies were popular, with a groom running alongside and a boy seated beside the owner-driver, and later types of vehicles included the brougham and the phaeton. The 1840 census showed that there were then on the island 170 four-wheeled and 44 two-wheeled carriages, 266 ponies and 77 carts. Horses were obtained from Australia, and John Cameron remarks that a stable of from one to twelve horses was owned by 'everyone', evidently meaning all European gentlemen. Annual horse sales were held in Commercial Square until 1886, when they ceased as a result of the amount of heavy traffic going through.

Complaints of traffic congestion came early and have always been frequent. A newspaper article of 1872 bemoaned the fact that no rule of the road had been laid down, with the result that bullock carts and gharries wandered about on either side, getting in the way of carriages and ponies, and causing vehicles to be tumbled into the monsoon ditches alongside. By the 1880s there were new hazards : the first rickshaws arrived from Shanghai in 1880 and multiplied rapidly, and we find a member of the legislative council referring to the 'noiseless but deadly bicycle'. In

1889, Rudyard Kipling found that 'in the city they run over you and jostle you into the kennel', and at the time of his visit there were steam trams to contend with. The trams, started in 1885, ran from the brickworks at Pasir Panjang Road through Telok Blangah and Keppel Road to the Tanjong Pagar docks, and thence to Collyer Quay. A branch line ran north to South Bridge Road, and through the town to end at Rochore. The Rochore section was closed in 1892 in response to increasing competition from rickshaws, and the steam trams were finally abandoned in 1894. Electric trams began running over similar routes in 1902, and continued until 1926, covering 15¾ miles of roadway.

The first motor car to reach Singapore was a 5hp vehicle imported at secondhand in 1896 by Katz Bros, representing Benz et Cie, and owned by C. B. Buckley, the author of *An Anecdotal History of Old Times in Singapore*. Known to irreverent members of the European community as 'the coffee machine', it reputedly required a teaspoonful of petrol put into the carburettor and lit with a match to warm it up, and could be started only by turning a large flywheel at the back of the car by hand. In the same year Mrs G. M. Dare became Singapore's first woman motorist, driving a 12hp Star, and the two other earliest cars in the colony were an Albion and a de Dion Bouton. It was another ten years or so before the new form of transport became widely accepted and replaced the gharry and rickshaw to any extent, but by March 1908 there were 214 people licensed to drive cars, motor-bicycles and steamrollers.

By 1925, there was again serious concern over traffic congestion, as taxis, buses and cars thronged the streets by day and at night were impeded by great numbers of empty rickshaws which their owners left out for want of depots in which to store them. A municipal bill of 1911 provided for the gradual disappearance of the double-seated rickshaw, on humanitarian grounds, but in the 1920s, though the seat had been made narrower, two passengers often squeezed in. During the Japanese occupation, bicycle-pulled trishaws gained ground, and these are still in use, though likely to disappear within the next decade, as the hand-drawn rickshaws did after the war. (The number of rickshaws, which in 1923 was about 10,000, began to fall in 1928; in 1941 there were 4,000.)

The first public motor transport company was the Singapore Traction Co, which initially operated trolley buses and omnibuses after the failure of Singapore Electric Tramways Ltd. The last trolley bus was taken off the road in December 1962. For several decades public transport facilities that were both swift and cheap were quite inadequate, and indeed, in 1936, British gunners stationed at Changi bought buses with which to start their own *Ubique* service to and from Singapore.

Soon after World War I, Chinese-owned 'mosquito' buses, built by attaching a body with seven seats to a motor-car chassis, began to operate, and became extremely popular : by 1927 there were 456. In 1935 they were amalgamated with the existing Chinese companies to form ten bus companies, and the trend moved in favour of larger buses. In April 1971 the government supervised a further reorganisation of the bus services, and they were amalgamated into four companies serving the four quarters of the island. At the same time, severe legislation was enacted against pirate taxis, which had taken much of the bus and legitimate taxi trade in the postwar period. The National Trades Union Congress simultaneously started a workers' transport co-operative, COMFORT, to enable taxi drivers to own their vehicles.

Total Vehicles on Register	665,873
Motor Cars : Private	142,568
Motor Cars : Public (1)	5,692
Motor Buses (2)	2,298
Goods Vehicles	34,119
Motor Cycles and Scooters	105,214
Bicycles	372,276
Trishaws	3,389
Road Rollers and Tractors	317

SINGAPORE VEHICLE REGISTRATION, DECEMBER 1970
(1) includes taxis, hired cars and tuition cars
(2) includes private motor buses

SINGAPORE

By 1971, Singapore had the second highest car population ratio in Asia, with one car to every sixteen people. By May 1821, about fifteen miles of roads had been made; by 1919 there were 119 miles; by 1970, 1,204 miles, including 847 with permanent surfaces and 357 unpaved *kampong* roads.

The two international routes of the Asian Highway in Cambodia, Laos, Vietnam, Thailand, West Malaysia and the south of the ECAFE region are now ready for ordinary vehicular traffic, and should lead to a rapid growth of road transport for purposes both of tourism and trade, in which Singapore will have a share.

Railways

The overland link with the mainland by both road and rail is the Causeway, originally completed in September 1923, and 3,465ft long. It carries a pipe bringing fresh water from Johore to Singapore, a 26ft-wide road, and a two-track railway. The average depth of water in which it was laid is 47ft at one point and 77ft at another, at low tide. The railway is part of the Malayan system, and after crossing the Causeway continues for a distance of 16 miles to the terminus station near Keppel Harbour.

The first railway in Singapore, opened on 1 January 1903, ran from Kranji to Pasir Panjang. The terminus station was at Tank Road for all passenger trains for many years, though an extension to Keppel Harbour was opened in 1907. The Kranji line ran from Telok Blangah over Craig Hill to People's Park, across the river by way of Pulau Saigon, and along Tank Road, Cuppage Road and Clemenceau Avenue to Newton Circus. It reached the Johore Straits in 1902, but even after the Peninsula line was completed in 1918, and trains were running from Johore to Bangkok, there was only a ferry until the building of the Causeway. Accommodation at Tank Road terminus proving inadequate, the line was diverted from Bukit Panjang, the old line abandoned, and the modern station built in 1932 at Tanjong Pagar. The Singapore portion of the line was bought by the Federated Malay States in 1912. Singapore is linked to Malaysia

108

and Thailand by regular day and night express train services. The line joins the Thailand frontier at Padang Besar and continues to Bangkok.

In 1928 a 1½ mile railway was built at Changi to transport exceptionally heavy loads from the pier to the gun batteries at the artillery side, with a loop line to serve the ammunition dump on the edge of the Selarang swamp. It was standard gauge, and all the rolling stock had to be brought from England. The locomotive was transported by junk from Singapore Harbour.

AIR TRAVEL

The first flight in Singapore was made over the race course at Farrer Park in 1910 by a Frenchman, M Feraudi, in an Antoinette monoplane, and the island's importance as a halfway house between continents was recognised anew when, in 1919, Captain Ross Smith landed in the centre of that same race course on his way from England to Australia. Pioneer aviators such as Alan Cobham, Bert Hinkler and Tommy Kingsford Smith used it as a port of call in the next few years, and it became a stop for many world air record attempts. The first airport, built at Seletar to defend the naval base, was in operation in the late twenties. The first civil aircraft to land there was *The Spirit of Australia*, piloted by Captain Hurley in 1928. Amy Johnson landed there in 1930 in her Gypsy Moth, and in the same year the first commercial flight into Singapore took place. The first air mail arrived in 1931, on a triple-engined Imperial Airways Hercules, *Cairo*. Seletar is still in use as a military airport, and is also a centre for oil and timber transport.

Kallang airport was opened in 1937, and made available for use by all types of aircraft, with the result that Singapore now became a recognised stop on world air routes. Kallang was used by the Japanese during the occupation, and they employed prisoner-of-war labour to build a new airfield at Changi, from which their planes began flying in 1944. The base at Changi was returned to the British Army at the end of the war, but handed over to the RAF in 1948. It became the main RAF headquarters, and the terminal point for the Transport Command York service from Britain. No 48 and later No 52 squadron operated transport routes throughout the Far East from Changi, and it was used, largely for supply-dropping, in anti-communist operations in Malaya from 1948 to 1957. From 1958, Shackletons were flown out to undertake research and rescue operations. Changi was handed over to the Singapore government at the end of 1971, as part of the British military withdrawal, for use as a civilian airport. There is another small military airfield at Tengah, also formerly owned by the British.

The facilities at Kallang were found inadequate after the war, and on 20 August 1955 a new international airport was opened at Paya Lebar, $7\frac{1}{2}$ miles from the city. Facilities have expanded and improved under a longterm plan of continuous development, and by 1971 it was regularly used by twenty-three international airlines in addition to Malaysia-Singapore Airlines (MSA). The airport received its first jumbo jet aircraft in 1971, and supersonic aircraft are expected in 1973. MSA was formed in May 1966 as a joint venture between the two countries, but in 1971 it was agreed that in 1973 they should run their airlines separately.

A more recent development in Singapore's role as a communications centre is the establishment of a charter airline, Saber, 80 per cent of which is owned by the government under an agreement with Overseas National Airways, an American company. The intention is to make Singapore a world centre of air cargo transport as well as setting up a passenger charter service bringing tourist groups in from other parts of the Far East.

POSTAL SERVICES

Facilities at Singapore were originally a branch of the Indian Post Office under the control of the director-general at Calcutta. The Master Attendant was locally responsible, and from 1836 on had to provide boats for the conveying of mail to and from steamers in the harbour. People watched the flagstaff keenly, since the signal for a ship to the eastward often signified mail arriving via Batavia. Nineteenth-century descriptions of European domestic life in Singapore are full of references to the way in which the women, condemned to a monotonous and trivial existence, lived for letters from home. In the 1820s, to receive an answer within nine months, says Buckley, was considered 'very punctual'. In 1845, mail was delivered by the P & O service from London in forty-one days; and once, in September 1854, in thirty-four days, which was thought quite remarkable.

There was no internal postal service for almost forty years, and even then all mail had to be taken to or claimed from a single post office, registers of all letters received being kept. In 1885 pre-pay postage stamps were introduced. These and all other stamps in use from 1855 to 1867 were issued in Calcutta by the East India Company. The first issue of distinctive Straits Settlements stamps took place on 1 September 1867. The first postal delivery service was restricted to the town, and horse-drawn mail coaches were used. The overland parcel post was opened on 1 April 1875, and extended to Britain on 1 October 1885. The first post office savings bank was opened in 1877, and the first sub post office dates from the turn of the century.

Singapore now has 42 post offices, 25 postal agencies, 2 mobile post offices and 58 stamp vendors. The Post Office undertakes many agency services for government departments, including the collection and payment of Central Provident Fund contributions, the payment of social welfare allowances, civil pensions and allowances, army and air force allowances, radio and television licences, the renewal of driving licences, the collection and payment of TOTO bets, and the sales of sweepstake tickets. Between 1959 and 1970, the number of postal articles annually handled doubled, and is now over 230 million. Over 40 million airmail items are handled annually, and direct airmail despatches are made to eighty-eight overseas offices of exchange. Singapore is now a principal distribution depot for Malaysia, Brunei, the Philippines and Indonesia. Locally, mail is delivered for the most part by bicycle or scooter, and in some cases by boat. The Singapore Post Office frequently makes new issues of stamps and first day covers.

TELECOMMUNICATIONS

Singapore has been a major regional and world centre of telecommunications since the early days of the telegraph system, owing to its geographical location and commercial importance. In 1863 a telegraph line linked the docks to the town. By 1914 Singapore radiated a network of telegraph cables to India, Ceylon, Java, Australia, Hong Kong and Indochina, and thence all over the world. In 1966 the government took over the Singapore assets of Cable & Wireless. The republic is now the westernmost terminus of the co-axial Commonwealth Telephone Cable System, extending from London via Canada and the Pacific, and of which SEACOM is the regional portion. In 1967 it was chosen as one of nine Category 1 Transit Centres in the International Telecommunications Union (ITU) Telephone World Routing Plan. It is also a members of the International Telecommunications Satellite Consortium (INTELSAT).

In 1971 a satellite earth station was installed on Sentosa, with an initial capacity of 132 telephone channels. It provides additional outlets to other similarly equipped countries via the Indian Ocean Satellite (INTELSAT III) westwards to Britain and eastwards to Western Australia and Japan. It connects telephone exchanges through the microwave station at Fort Canning, and receives telecasts direct from Japan and Europe.

Singapore holds fourth position within the British Commonwealth in the volume of telegraph traffic handled, and sixth position in the volume of international telephone and telex calls. Between 30 and 40 per cent of its telegraph traffic is transit traffic. An automatic national telex exchange came into operation in 1971, and its aeronautical telegraph communications are already semi-automatic. A coast station has been established for radio-telephone and radio-telegraph communication with ships in mid-ocean all over the world. Medium range maritime telephone equipment has been installed to assist communication with the offshore oil rigs.

TELEPHONE SERVICE

The first telephone was installed in 1879, and Singapore was one of the first cities in the Far East to use it. A fifty-line switchboard was introduced by the local manager of the then Eastern Extension Telegraph Company on the first floor of the Paterson Simon and Company Building in Prince Street. (Prince Street was obliterated under the urban renewal programme in 1971 : it ran from Collyer Quay to de Souza Street.) The first public telephone service was set up by the Oriental Telephone & Electric Co Ltd in Robinson Road in February 1881, and operated sixty lines linking prominent commercial firms. In 1900 the company allowed the Tanjong Pagar Dock Company to organise its own telephone system. In 1905 the company moved to Hill Street, which became the site of the main exchange. By this time over a thousand lines were in operation and overhead wires were being replaced by underground cabling.

During the bombing of 1942 and the subsequent Japanese occupation, 5,000 of Singapore's 11,000 telephones were destroyed or lost, and the cable network was badly damaged and never properly maintained. After the war the service was restored by the Oriental Telephone & Electric Co Ltd, but the supply of new telephones did not keep pace with demand. On 1 January 1955 the Singapore government took over the company's assets, and the Singapore Telephone Board was established as a corporation by special ordinance. The number of telephone instruments with subscribers rose in the next fifteen years from 34,500 to 161,000 and the number of public telephones from 100 to 900. In the number of telephones per 100 of population, Singapore, with 7·6, comes third in East Asia behind Japan (22) and Hong Kong (12). Under the STB's 1971–5 development plan, the percentage will rise to 15 by the end of 1975, at which time there will be 216,000 lines in existence, and 325,000 instruments connected to the board's system.

Singapore now has twelve public exchanges, linked by underground cable, and by 1975 the number will have been increased to twenty-three. Subscriber Trunk Dialling (STD), introduced in 1962 as an experiment, was fully implemented in 1965, and Singapore subscribers can dial direct to Kuala Lumpur, Malacca, Ipoh, and Penang. In April 1968 the Pulse Code Modulation (PCM) was introduced, and installed in the Katong-Changi circuit. Singapore is among the first countries in South East Asia to use PCM in cable transmission. International telephone calls are available to 141 countries.

METEOROLOGY

Singapore is an important international relay centre for meteorological information with the northern and southern hemispheres on behalf of the World Meteorological Organisation. The earliest meteorological observations were made by the first Resident, William Farquhar, between 1820 and 1825 in an *attap* shed on Fort Canning. In 1840 the East India Company sent Lieutenant Charles Morgan Elliot to establish a Singapore observatory, and he made observations until the end of 1845 from a hut at the mouth of the Kallang River. In January 1869 such observations were again undertaken on the orders of the Colonial Office, but all the early records were made with simple instruments, and mainly concerned straightforward weather statistics.

A full scale meteorological station was established at Mount Faber only in January 1929, with the coming of regular air traffic into Singapore. It was moved to Kallang airport in 1934 and to Paya Lebar in 1955. An upper air observatory, established soon after World War II, now has sophisticated weather-radar and weather-satellite cloud-picture receiving equipment. It is operated by the government Meteorological Department, which has in addition a climatological section, a port meteorological section, a first order meteorological station, a weather forecast office and a network of rainfall stations. It spends most of its time gathering information for air and sea transport, and is expanding rapidly as a result of increasing government responsibility for civil and military aviation since the British withdrawal.

RADIO AND TELEVISION

The first wireless station in Singapore was hurriedly set up in 1914 on the outbreak of war, by the Eastern Extension Company, in order to communicate with ships in the harbour. The first commercial wireless station was opened at Paya Lebar on 8 October 1915, and was controlled by the Post Office. By 1923, amateurs were operating from two experimental stations, and the Radio Society of Singapore was formed in 1925. The first large-scale commercial radio station was the British Malayan Broadcasting Corporation, established in 1936 in Singapore. In 1940 it was taken over by the Government of the Straits Settlements, and a newly created Department of Broadcasting was set up on 1 April 1946. Nowadays, radio and television services are the responsiblity of the Ministry of Culture. Radio services in the four official languages are put out on separate channels in the medium wave, short wave and FM bands, all of which broadcast commercials though, as on television, these are restricted to certain types of programme. Normally, Malay and Chinese programmes are each broadcast from 5am to midnight, English from 6am to midnight and Tamil from 5am to 9pm, after which this channel is used until midnight for Chinese broadcasts in seven dialects: Mandarin, Hokkien, Cantonese, Teochew, Hakka, Foochew, and Hainanese. Radio Singapore has by far the highest density of listeners in South East Asia, and more than 70 per cent of the population tune in daily.

115

SINGAPORE

Television began as a pilot service from 6pm to 7.30pm on Channel 5 on 15 February 1963, and a permanent TV centre was completed in 1966. TV programmes in four languages are put out on two channels on the CCIR characteristic and 625 lines per frame 50c/s system in the VHF Band III. Subtitles in a second official language are used for films. Both radio and television are of the greatest importance as channels of government information and ways of presenting the various cultures of Singapore to each other's attention. Well-known British and American television series are shown in addition to films from India, Indonesia and Hong Kong, and locally produced features of all kinds. With such a variety of languages, it is difficult to please everyone, and complaints that Tamil, for example, is not being given its due are fairly frequent, but in fact each language is given a certain percentage of radio and TV time. By 1971, 240,000 radio and TV licences were being issued annually.

PRESS

The *Singapore Chronicle*, started in 1824, was Singapore's first newspaper, and was followed in 1835 by the *Singapore Free Press*, which survived as a weekly until 1869. The *Straits Times*, Singapore's oldest newspaper, started in 1845, has been published twice weekly from 1847, and daily from 1858. There were no newspapers in languages other than English until the end of rule from India in 1867, and the first three Chinese daily newspapers were published in 1881, 1890 and 1898 respectively.

Singapore now supports 4 Chinese daily newspapers, 2 English daily newspapers, 1 Malay daily newspaper, 3 Tamil daily newspapers and 1 Malayalam newspaper. Some of these papers, including the *Straits Times*, are on sale in Malaysia. The highest daily circulations within Singapore among the Chinese papers are those of the *Nanyang Siang Pau* and *Sin Chew Jit Poh*, and among the English-language papers the leader in the *Straits Times*

116

(105,000). The Malay *Berita Harian* averages about 12,800 and the *Tamil Merasu* 7,100.

The question of newspaper censorship has been a vexed one since independence. The government allows considerable freedom of speech, but on a few occasions, as in 1971, has made arrests and brought pressure on editors to secure conformity on what it regards as sensitive issues, usually those with a racial connotation. Two English-language papers, the *Eastern Sun* and the *Singapore Herald*, ceased publication in 1971 as a result of government action, while four senior executives of the *Nanyang Siang Pau* were detained without charge.

6 GOVERNMENT

THE system of government in Singapore is parliamentary and voting is compulsory for all citizens of twenty-one years of age and over, regardless of sex, race or creed, income or educational qualifications. Members of Parliament are elected by simple majority in single-member constituencies; in 1970, they included 42 Chinese, 7 Indians, 5 Malays and 2 Eurasians. In 1971, a bill was drawn up to change the electoral boundaries, and to increase the number of constituencies from 58 to 65, the reasons given being the increase in population and the movement consequent on the vast re-development and building programmes. The People's Action Party (PAP), led by Lee Kuan Yew, won all seats at the 1968 election, and has been in power since the first fully elected legislative assembly was returned in 1959.

Parliament is elected for a period of five years, and there are no scheduled dates for its meetings, which are open to the public. Its rules of procedure closely follow those of the British Parliament at Westminster, and it is presided over by a speaker, elected by Parliament as an additional member not himself qualified to vote. All four official languages may be used during parliamentary debates, and simultaneous translations are provided for members of the public as well as members of the house. In practice, English is generally employed, though recently there has been some challenge to its supremacy by members choosing to speak Mandarin.

The head of state is the president, elected by parliament for a term of four years. The functions of his office are symbolic rather

118

Page 119 A street in Chinatown: note the trishaw, the hawkers' stalls, and the goods laid out for sale on a cloth, centre foreground. The pillars of the five-foot way, right, bear the names of the shops in Chinese characters

Page 120 (above) Government Housing Development Board flats at Toa Payoh; tenants and owner-occupiers include a wide range of blue-collar and white-collar workers; *(below)* the power station at Pasir Panjang, until recently adequate to Singapore's needs: industrial development has made the building of a new 600mW power station at Jurong, to be completed in 1973, a matter of urgency

than political, and may perhaps be compared to those of European monarchs like the English and Dutch, who provide in their official image a focus for nationhood. Singapore's first President, Yusof bin Ishak, who died in 1970, was a Malay, and his appointment was clearly in tune with the conciliatory policy of declaring Malay as Singapore's national language. His successor, President Benjamin Sheares, a Eurasian surgeon with a Chinese wife, has never participated in political affairs. Real power is in the hands of the prime minister and the eleven other ministers of the cabinet. Four of these men in the PAP government are of especial significance as policymakers and spokesmen: Lee himself, Dr Goh Keng Swee, Dr Toh Chin Chye, and Mr S. Rajaratnam.

Mr Lee Kuan Yew, the Prime Minister, is a Chinese of Hakka origin. Educated at Raffles Institution and at Cambridge, Lee became a lawyer on his return from England, and acted as legal adviser to several trade union organisations. He is fluent in Mandarin, Hokkien, English and Malay. The details of his career are set out in Alex Josey's biography.

Dr Goh Keng Swee, Minister of Defence 1965–7 and again from 1970, has nevertheless spent most of his cabinet life as Minister of Finance, and has had a strong influence on Singapore's economic policies. Dr Toh Chin Chye, Chairman of the PAP, Vice-Chancellor of the University of Singapore, and in 1970 Minister for Science and Technology, known to the public perhaps more for his tough line on student politics than for anything else, is the third Chinese. Mr S. Rajaratnam, the Minister for Foreign Affairs and Labour, a former journalist and an extremely able speaker, is of Sinhalese-Indian extraction.

The other eight cabinet ministers include a Malay, a Eurasian and six more Chinese, the Chinese representing between them the Hakka, the Hokkien and the Cantonese elements. The cabinet is remarkable for the fact that about half its members have been continuously in power, though sometimes with a change in portfolio, since the PAP government took office in 1959. This continuity has clearly given to the leadership, which has sometimes

H

121

been described as a benevolent dictatorship, the kind of strength often lacking in other democratically elected governments. The PAP government exercises fairly tight control over the press, trade unions, and student bodies, and a number of communist political detainees, probably about seventy, are held without trial. Having been given a mandate by the people, Lee Kuan Yew and his government show no hesitation in acting as they personally think best for the future of Singapore. There is, for example, no appeal against compulsory national service, and all incoming publications, films and gramophone records are subject to censorship, though this is comparatively liberal, except where communist propaganda, racial confrontation and the hippie cult are concerned.

Lee Kuan Yew and his cabinet obviously recognise the dangers of inflexibility and of hardening of the political arteries, though, in common with all governments, they have not always managed to avoid it. A political study centre was set up to bring the civil service out of the colonial era in its ways of thinking and direct it towards the needs of an independent multi-racial society: all senior civil servants attended courses there. It was closed down in 1969, having served its purpose. A special council, the Majlis Ugama Singapura, advises the government on Muslim religious matters. Intensive study of particular problems and exposure to what is going on in other countries are combined in the 'sabbaticals' which Lee Kuan Yew enables some of his cabinet ministers to take in foreign universities. The Minister for Culture studied at Cambridge and at the London School of Economics in 1969–70; and in 1970–1 the Minister for Home Affairs was at Princeton.

There are no subordinate forms of government below Parliament: separate local government authorities were eliminated in June 1959. Since 1966, Citizens' Consultative Committees have been established in all electoral constituencies, grouped into three rural district committees and five city district committees for administrative purposes, and each having a civil servant,

122

responsible to the prime minister's office, as its *ex officio* head. Through these committees, grievances are brought to government attention and official policies explained to the people. By this means the government keeps a finger on the nation's pulse and possibly a restraining grip on any potential enemy's wrist.

In April 1970 the first appointments were made to a newly constituted presidential council. Members are appointed by the president on the advice of the cabinet, ten of them for life and a further ten for a period of three years. The proceedings are conducted in private. Not all members have been appointed, it being thought desirable to reserve some places for possible members from a future government. The council's function is to send back to Parliament for further consideration any legislation which in its opinion threatens the rights of any minority. Such rights being of necessity an extremely delicate matter for discussion in Singapore's multi-racial setting, Parliament decreed that bills certified by the prime minister as being urgent and necessary to meet emergencies would be exempted from such consideration. The current position is, therefore, that in the last resort the prime minister has virtually unlimited powers, yet at the end of Parliament's five-year term may find himself and his party rejected at the polls.

In fact, it is difficult to see where effective political opposition is to come from. Avowed communists are imprisoned or in exile; David Marshall's Workers' Party is defunct, the Barisan Sosialis has boycotted Parliament since October 1966. There have been, nevertheless, one or two recent attempts to start a new party.

There is no doubt that the PAP government has shown remarkable efficiency in solving Singapore's economic problems and in inculcating a national sense of discipline. The republic's small size makes it comparatively easy to enforce legislation, providing it does not cut across matters of racial and cultural pride, but the same fact discourages political discussion: voices echo more loudly, speakers are more conspicuous in a confined space. The government often states its wish to benefit from some kind of critical opposition, but it is difficult for the people to know where

123

the limits are set, as was revealed by the difficulties in 1971 over the question of newspaper censorship. This presents a very real problem for the government, the leaders of which, it may be added, are outstanding in their lack of corruption and personal ostentation. Its chief internal political problems are concerned with the multi-racial nature of society and with the differences in outlook between the Chinese-educated and the English-educated sections of the Chinese population. External threats may come from mainland communism or from anti-Chinese elements in the surrounding Malay nations. Singapore's economic and social progress is such as to arouse considerable envy in less advanced countries.

LAW

The system, based largely on English common law, with modifications to meet local customs, was laid down by Raffles as a general principle in the early years of the settlement. The first magistrate was appointed in 1823, and an interesting sign of early multi-racialism is that juries of five Europeans or 'four Europeans and three respectable natives' were instituted. At first the Resident conducted his own court, but this was closed in 1827, and a court of judicature for the Straits Settlements was opened, with a peripatetic judge. Before this time, there was no means of affording redress against Europeans in civil cases, and nothing to be done against them in criminal matters, short of sending them before the supreme court in Calcutta. Singapore's first criminal sessions were opened in 1828 and its first executions quickly followed. In 1864, the governor was given the power of banishment, but this applied only to aliens, not to British subjects.

The modern judiciary is free from overt interference by the executive or legislative branches of government; the chief justice is appointed by the president after consultation with the prime minister. Judges serve until the age of sixty-five, and may be removed only by the recommendation of a tribunal of other judges of the supreme court on grounds of misbehaviour or in-

124

competence. The supreme court consists of a high court, a court of appeal and a court of criminal appeal, but the judicial committee of the privy council in London constitutes the final court of appeal. The district courts try civil cases involving sums of not more than $2,000 (£272; US $666), criminal offences for which the maximum penalty is not more than seven years' imprisonment and, where the public prosecutor applies and the accused consent, offences punishable with death or life imprisonment. The magistrates' courts have power only to try criminal offences for which the maximum penalty is not more than three years.

In 1959, despite keen local controversy, the government succeeded in putting through legislation abolishing trial by jury for all cases except those involving the death penalty, arguing that the jury system had never worked well in the Singapore context. In 1969 the abolition was extended to cover all contingencies. The Minister for Law declared at the time that the government was not willing to 'allow justice to be thwarted through either squeamishness or ignorance'. Capital charges are now heard by two judges, who must achieve unanimity to convict on the original charge. Singapore retains execution by hanging for capital crimes, and corporal punishment is a commonplace.

A legal aid bureau was set up in 1958, but is so far very limited in its application, since few people qualify and aid in criminal cases extends only to capital offences. A central complaints bureau was set up in 1962 to investigate public complaints concerning the conduct of public servants in the execution of their duties.

A special feature of the legal system is the Shariah Court, which is open to the public, has English and Malay as its languages, and deals only with matters of marriage, divorce and inheritance affecting Muslim citizens, which are administered according to Muslim law. For details the reader is referred to the books of Judith Djamour. In all other fields, Muslim Singaporeans come under the same laws as those of other religions. Polygynous unions, common among Muslims of other countries and traditional to Chinese culture, though in the form of concubinage, now have no legal force except in very rare cases of Muslim marriage, for which in Singapore the first wife must give her permission. This result was achieved by the Women's Charter, enacted on 15 September 1961, which, however, left undisturbed polygynous unions legally recognised before this date. The charter also abolished divorce by mutual consent, practised by many Chinese and some Hindus as well as by Muslims, and all marriages are now dissolved only by a court order.

Slavery

Slavery had long been a commonplace in the territories surrounding Singapore, and in Singapore itself it survived in various forms for many years. In the early days of the British settlement, Bugis traders imported boy and girl slaves annually and are said to have sold them at the riverside, close to the Resident's house, and to have offered them as presents both to the Resident and to Raffles himself.

Raffles formally prohibited slavery, putting into effect an act of parliament, in 1823 : he himself had heard kidnapped women calling for assistance from a boat in the river. The legislation applied only to the future and did not free those who were already slaves. John Crawfurd, the Resident, had considerable difficulty with the Temenggong and the sultan, who claimed that slavery was permitted under Malayan law, and who treated virtually all their followers as slaves : in 1824, twenty-seven pretty young female slaves from the sultan's harem sought refuge at the police office, where they showed the marks of cruel treatment. The sultan was beyond the jurisdiction of Crawfurd, who allowed the women to go free.

In later years, slavery resolved itself into two specific forms : debt-slavery and the prostitution of women who were bought or kidnapped in Cochin China or in China itself and brought to Singapore. The Temenggong and the sultan numbered many debt-slaves among their followers in the early years; later, coolies

126

arriving from China pledged their labour in return for their passage, and in 1873 W. H. Read refers to the fact that many of Singapore's Boyanese syces and gardeners were debt-slaves, paying off the cost of their pilgrimage to Mecca.

In addition to the women imported solely to act as prostitutes, young blind girls were bought in China and old women led them through the streets at night to sing for anyone who called for them : there are several references between 1880 and 1910 to the moral dangers they ran, and in 1908 they were forbidden to perform on licensed premises. The Chinese system of *mui tsai* ('little sister') adoptions led to many abuses, as in the case of a girl of sixteen, which came before the courts in 1907. She had been bought for $230, made to work nineteen hours a day, and flogged, hung up by the hair, or pricked about the face with needles when her owners were angry. Such adoptions were not made illegal until the 1930s and, although the system was intended to give girls from poor families a home and a chance of marriage, it was subject to severe abuse.

The position of women

The social and economic position of women in Singapore is tremendously varied. There are numbers of women, mostly Chinese, Indian and Ceylonese, in the professions, an outstanding example being Mrs Lee Kuan Yew, who practises as a 'lawyer's lawyer' and whose duties do not require her to appear in the public courts. At the same time, mainly because of the close family ties still traditional in the East, there is nothing that could be described as a women's liberation movement, and indeed the work of professionally qualified women is in most cases made possible by the efforts of a large band of servants, mostly female and often illiterate. By 1970, only about 20 per cent of women above the age of fifteen worked at other than domestic tasks; with rising standards of education and the trend towards labour-saving machines, the position of women is moving nearer to that of their western sisters, and this percentage may be expected to increase substantially. Nearly all women in the professions receive equal pay with men doing the same work.

Many traditional attitudes are firmly retained and are reflected in legislation such as that covering national service, which affects only males. There are provisions for the training of female volunteers, but there is no question of girls being called up to work side by side with young soldiers and to live away from home for more than a night or two at a time. Nevertheless, the right of women to decide the size of their family has been legally recognised to some extent, as in the Abortion Act of 1969, which enables pregnancy to be terminated by registered doctors on humanitarian grounds and generally on the authority of the Termination of Pregnancy Authorisation Board. The act was brought into operation for an experimental period of five years. Voluntary sterilisation in certain circumstances was legalised at the same time.

CRIME AND THE POLICE

The incidence of crime in Singapore throughout the nineteenth century was probably much higher than it need have been because of the poor condition of the police force. In 1819 the first Master Attendant, Francis Bernard, was put in charge of the police, and in 1821 had a staff of 2 sergeants and 17 constables. By 1841 the force consisted of 3 European constables, 1 assistant, 14 officers and 110 policemen, almost all of them Klings from the South of India, with some Malays. All were untrained and extremely badly paid. Consequently they were very vulnerable to bribery, and throughout the nineteenth century there were complaints of the force's inefficiency and corruption. The main cause of crime, as of police corruption, was gambling, to which both Chinese and Malays were addicted, and which went on openly for years despite legislation against it.

Some improvement was made after the appointment of Thomas Dunman as superintendent of police in 1843. He became the first commissioner of police in 1857, and was the first to organise

128

them properly and to inculcate pride in their calling. Nevertheless they continued to be overworked and underpaid, and Governor Blundell complained in 1858 that they did not receive 'so much as ordinary domestic servants . . . and far less than ordinary seamen'. Well-to-do citizens kept their own bodies of watchmen, and on occasion, as at a time of serious secret society riots, acted as special constables.

In 1881 the first police school was started, and European-trained constables and a large contingent of Sikhs arrived for duty. A separate detective force was first organised in 1884, and a criminal registration department set up in 1901. A fingerprint system was introduced in 1903. The police were put into a uniform of blue serge coat and white drill trousers about 1863, but khaki was substituted in 1893. Today the police have reverted to navy blue.

The modern police force numbers over 6,000 regulars, assisted by 1,200 guide and escort personnel, about 800 volunteer constables and nearly 9,000 national servicemen. Women police include an assistant superintendent, 4 senior officers and 291 junior officers. The force is organised under the criminal investigation department, the traffic police, and the police reserve units, which help in the quelling of riots and civil disturbances and assist with crime prevention patrols. The whole of the island is patrolled by a network of police radio cars, and the harbour and territorial waters are watched by the marine police in their launches. Their main duties are to check smuggling and the introduction of illegal immigrants.

Singapore's early years, as might be expected, gave rise to some dramatic crimes. The first Resident, Colonel William Farquhar, in 1822 narrowly escaped assassination when he was stabbed by a disgruntled Malay. His assailant was cut down by Farquhar's son, and the body, after being sent round the town in a buffalo cart preceded by a man beating a gong, was hung up in an iron cage at Telok Ayer, on the orders of Raffles. In 1875 the prison superintendent was killed during a mass breakout at the jail, and in 1887 Walter Pickering, of the Chinese protectorate, was attacked and badly injured by a Chinese wielding an axe.

In 1832 there was a public complaint, via the grand jury, of 'the numerous burglaries that had been committed by gangs of Chinese in bodies of 50–100 men'. Things had evidently not improved much by 1846, when a gang of 200 Chinese attacked the house of one Mr Hewetson, about two miles from the town. As usual in those pioneering days, a neighbour came to the victim's aid, but he was badly beaten, and the police did not arrive until some time after the robbers had left with their plunder.

Over the years there were a number of murders. Number 70 North Bridge Road became the scene of three curiously similar crimes: in 1887, 1895 and 1918 respectively, a Russian Jewess was killed on the premises; all three were strangled, and two had been beaten with an iron bolt. The Pole convicted for the first of these murders was found wandering three days later, distraught and half-naked, and claimed that the house was bewitched. A Chinese servant was convicted of the third assault. More commonplace were cases of *amok*, which still occasionally occur: one of the worst took place in 1863 when a Javanese sailor killed three people, wounded three others, and set a house on fire before being shot by a police inspector.

Nevertheless, apart from secret society riots, Singapore, in the later years of the nineteenth and in the twentieth century, has had a relatively low crime rate. Robbery, housebreaking, forgery and embezzlement, usually closely connected with gambling, were the common crimes, as they are today. Sexual crime, it was remarked at the time of Singapore's centenary in 1919, was singular for its absence, though reference has already been made to the brothel slaves of earlier years, and in 1882 Mr Bond, speaking in the legislative council, remarked darkly that 'We must face facts . . . and one is that if there is an inadequate supply of females in this Colony, an abominable state of affairs comes into existence which should not be allowed'. Roland Braddell, writing in 1934, recalls that all the European *maisons tolérées* were closed

130

during World War I, principally because their inhabitants were of enemy nationality, and laments that since 1930 'a rigid campaign of suppression has been forced upon us by enthusiasts in England and elsewhere'. Modern Singapore, unlike other great ports of the world, to some extent retains this puritanical character, though its Bugis Street is widely known as a haunt of prostitutes, many of them male transvestites, and its nightclubs feature ever more daring striptease shows, most of them imported from Europe.

Gang warfare has continued into modern times, though it is less important than it was in the 1920s and 1930s. In 1927, reference was made at a meeting of the legislative council to 'the continued activities of gunmen', and shooting in broad daylight was common, though there is reason to believe that many of the crimes were committed by Cantonese only recently arrived in Singapore. Secret society gangs continued in the interwar period to take responsibility for most of Singapore's organised crime : in 1921, for example, there were over a hundred gang robberies. R. C. H. McKie, writing in *This Was Singapore* of the period from 1937 to 1939, remarks that 'in recent years, rising unemployment, social insecurity, and the war between China and Japan led to a flare in gangsterism'. After World War II, robbery, smuggling and gun-running continued on a large scale for some time, and among the gangs there flourished a band of Malays who were expert cat-burglars.

Today the activities of the secret societies, though often murderous, are somewhat less of a problem. After World War II the traditional form of the secret society underwent some change. With smaller numbers of immigrants from China, the societies threw their membership open to other dialect groups. By 1948 there were imitative societies in other racial groups, such as the Malay *Merah-Puteh* society and the Indian MGR. (The MGR began as a fan club devoted to an Indian film star known only by these initials, but a minority of its members used it as a cover for extortion.) As time went on the Chinese societies ceased to

131

be the traditional refuge of the working man, and became rather a banding together of unemployed youths engaged in protection and extortion rackets affecting hawkers, small shopkeepers and prostitutes. Most of these youths were westernised in their tastes, and affected tattoos, code names, signs and particular ways of wearing their clothes and hair. The old triad loyalties, of 'all for one and one for all' disappeared.

Nevertheless, in the early 1960s Singapore saw a murder a week on average, and at least one in four was committed by secret-society fighting men using knives, bearing scrapers or acid bombs. Nineteen-sixty was a peak year for kidnapping—twenty persons were held to ransom, and three of them, all millionaires, were killed, two of them in offering resistance, one after being bound and gagged. Such kidnappings continue, though considerably fewer in numbers today, and some rich Chinese in Singapore go nowhere without bodyguards.

Offences							*Number of Arrests*
Murder	.	.	.	.	.	.	38
Voluntarily Causing Hurt/Grievous Hurt		.	.	.			59
Robberies (all kinds)	.	.	.	.	.		95
Housebreaking and Theft	.	.	.	.	.		69
Housebreakings (Attempts)	.	.	.	.	.		10
Other Thefts	.	.	.	.	.	.	466
Motor Vehicle Thefts	.	.	.	.	.		26
Bicycle Thefts	.	.	.	.	.		20
Criminal Breach of Trust	.	.	.	.	.		29
Cheating	.	.	.	.	.	.	16
Rape	.	.	.	.	.	.	12
Possession of Offensive Weapons	.	.	.	.	.		35

CRIME RATES
(January–June 1970)

Narcotics

The use of narcotics in the form of opium was not officially frowned on until relatively recent years. The colonial government farmed out the sale of opium throughout the nineteenth century, and Cameron remarks on the number of opium shops in the 1860s, their windows and doors screened off from the street. From time to time, as in 1895, government inquiries into the use of opium were instituted, and their reports invariably expressed confidence in the *status quo*. A slight change was made in 1909, when an opium commission recommended that the system of farming opium should be abolished and that the government monopoly of its preparation and distribution in the form of *chandu*, a black treacly fluid, should be substituted, but the sale of *chandu* was not prohibited until 1946. In the early 1960s, it was estimated that there were still about 10,000 opium addicts, but most of them were well into middle age and were heavy labourers or trishaw drivers who had taken to the habit for relief from their physical sufferings.

Today, Singapore continues to some extent to be a transit base for traffic in raw opium, though the problem is not very considerable. An occasional addict may be seen tottering about in the overcrowded areas of Chinatown or the Sungei Road market, but this is rare. There has been, however, an increase in illicit imports of *ganja* (marijuana) in recent years, and in September 1971 hashish was found on a freighter in the harbour—the first occasion in modern times when it has been discovered in Singapore. The same year saw the beginning of an intensive government effort against the introduction and the use of drugs : for the first time, there seemed to be real cause for alarm about drug-taking by young people, and the number of *ganja* addicts was estimated at about 3,000.

A narcotics bureau was set up to co-ordinate the work of the CID and the Customs, plans were made for a counselling service to advise parents, and foreigners known to be drug addicts or traffickers were summarily expelled. An educational campaign against drug addiction and abuse was promoted in the schools, and police patrols picked up and photographed youths with long hair, the Minister for Home Affairs remarking in explanation that 'It is significant that none of those picked up by the police for taking *ganja* in Singapore had short hair.'

SINGAPORE

Prisons

The first jail built in Singapore was for transported Indian convicts, and was in Queen Street. The first for local criminals was built, about 1823, on the site of the present central police station in South Bridge Road, which was at that time a swamp. The building gradually sank, so that eventually all the prisoners were put into what had been the upper storey. The surrounding wall sank too, to the point where debtors incarcerated there were able to step over it to take the Sunday evening walk permitted them. A new jail was built in 1847. In the 1860s, the remarkable Major McNair, Superintendent of Convicts and Executive Engineer, ran the criminal jail for a time with the help of only one European warder, the rest of the petty officers being recruited from among the prisoners, who numbered some 3,000. About this time there began the tradition, revived in recent years, whereby the prisoners made various articles, including rattan furniture, for sale to the public.

The present prison population of Singapore fluctuates around 5,000–6,000. As in most countries, the prisons are overcrowded and understaffed, but, unlike many other countries in Asia, Singapore's prisons are clean, and the prisoners are well fed and permitted to earn small amounts whilst being trained in a variety of manual skills. Prison industries include woodwork, metalwork, steam laundering, printing, bookbinding, tailoring, shoemaking, canework, timber processing and cement industries. At Changi there is a maximum security prison for those with sentences of twelve months or over, and other jails include a remand prison for short-term prisoners and young offenders; a reformative training centre for delinquents under the age of twenty-one; Woodlands open prison; and the female prison, which seldom has more than fifty inmates.

The penal settlement formerly run on Pulau Senang, with accommodation for 500, was closed down after the riot of 12 July 1963, and has not been re-opened. During the riot, which took place immediately after the prisoners had been issued with

134

tools for gardening, 200 convicts killed three prison officers and wounded all but one of the thirty warders. The superintendent's eyes were gouged out, he was hacked to death, and finally thrown into the flames of the radio room, which the convicts had set on fire. About one-third of the convicts on the island stood back and refused to take part in the riots, which appear to have been organised by secret-society leaders in a bid for escape. In 1965, eighteen of the former convicts were executed at Changi prison for the murders committed in the course of the outbreak.

There is a small aftercare department in the Ministry of Social Affairs for those convicted and put on probation, and for those released from the reformative training centre between the ages of $16\frac{1}{2}$ and 21. There is, however, no equivalent organisation for adults, and they are helped by the Singapore Aftercare Association, a voluntary body which runs a hostel and receives $8,000 (£1,080; US $2,700) annually from the government. Traditional attitudes of harshness and neglect persist among the public in general, despite the appointment of a small number of voluntary probation officers. The government itself refuses to employ ex-convicts except as labourers.

DEFENCE

Volunteer military service in Singapore dates back to 1854, when, partly as a result of the recent secret society riots, and partly because of the outbreak of the Crimean war, a volunteer rifle corps was formed. This was the first local volunteer corps in the British Empire, and consequently took as its motto 'in oriente primus'. It served in World War I, taking over garrison duties from the regular forces.

In 1922, the volunteer army in Singapore was integrated with the Straits Settlements Volunteer Force. The Straits Settlements Royal Navy Volunteer Reserve (SSRNVR) was formed in April 1934, and the Malayan Volunteer Air Force in 1939. In World War II, all elements of the volunteer forces participated in the

135

defence of Singapore, as far as they were able in the chaotic conditions prevailing. The volunteer corps was disbanded in June 1946, as a temporary measure, but was re-formed as the First Battalion Singapore Volunteer Corps, supported by a light AA battery, the Singapore Royal Artillery, the Armoured Car Squadron, Coastal Battery, Fire Command Battery, Field Engineer Squadron, Signal Squadron, Army Service Corps and Singapore Women's Auxiliary Corps. In 1947 the naval volunteer force was re-activated and named the Malayan Royal Naval Volunteer Reserve, and in 1950 the volunteer air force was re-organised as the Singapore wing of the Malayan Auxiliary Air Force.

National service was introduced on a limited scale by the colonial government in 1954, and 400 youths, chosen by ballot, were called up for military training. They were eventually posted to various units of the Singapore military forces to complete three years' service. Some of them served during the Emergency and as part of the Malaysian army in Sabah and West Malaysia. The first regular infantry battalion was formed on 12 March 1957, and received its colours in 1961 from the *Yang di-Pertuan Negara*. A second battalion was formed in 1962, and this, working closely with the police force, helped to restore law and order during the riots in 1964. Both battalions saw service in Sabah and were active during *konfrontasi*.

In August 1965, when Singapore became for the first time a fully independent sovereign state, after separation from Malaysia, the armed forces consisted of the First and Second Battalions of the Singapore Infantry Regiment, a volunteer artillery battery, and elements of signals and engineers, plus a naval unit of one patrol craft. The task of setting up a military force which would present a real deterrent to any potential enemy was thus considerable.

The Ministry of Interior and Defence was formed in November 1965, with Dr Goh Keng Swee as minister. In 1970 the ministry was split into two: the Ministry of Defence (MINDEF) and

Page 137 (above) Reclamation in progress at Tanjong Rhu; (below) Nicoll Highway, built on reclaimed land, with Merdeka Bridge and the Rochore River at right

Page 138 (above) Interior, Thian Hok Keng temple, Telok Ayer Street: over forty per cent of Singapore's Chinese are of Hokkien origin, and this is their most important place of worship; (below) the Sultan Mosque, Singapore's largest, took four years to build; it was opened in 1928 on the site of a mosque of the 1820s

the Ministry of Home Affairs, the latter dealing with police administration and problems of internal security. From 1965 onwards, the aim was to build up a nucleus of regular soldiers backed by a large reserve force, all of them trained to a high standard and supported by the most modern weapons and equipment. Emphasis in training and organisation of military forces is on flexibility, skill and speed. The Ministry of Defence is the supreme military headquarters which co-ordinates the deployment of the various units in the army, navy and air force, though command headquarters have been established to organise the different branches of the services. The headquarters and command structure are thus organised for all practical purposes on a single service basis. The Ministry of Defence has five major divisions: general staff; manpower; logistics; security and intelligence; and home affairs.

Singapore receives advice and training in military matters and the building up of armed forces from the State of Israel. In the early days after separation from Malaysia, the first Singapore Infantry Brigade was formed by the amalgamation of the two regular infantry regiments and the mobilised volunteer army. National service was introduced by the PAP in 1967, and all able-bodied men of eighteen years of age are called up. They are directed into fulltime service for two years, and all those selected for training as officers and all non-commissioned officers of the rank of corporal and above serve an additional six months, after which all pass into the reserve force, and do up to forty days' fulltime training annually for a further ten years. National servicemen are in general brought up to the standard of regular soldiers, and undergo additional training, as anti-riot squads, to meet any threat of internal subversion. Under this system, an infantry battalion in fulltime service reproduces itself every two years into a reserve battalion, and already six infantry battalions have been raised and organised into two infantry brigades; an armoured unit, using AMX tanks and V200s, has been formed. By 1979, under the present rate of enlistment, thirty infantry battalions will be formed as reserves, providing 45,000 trained soldiers on immediate mobilisation.

The Singapore Armed Forces Training Institute (SAFTI), originally the Jurong Military School, set up in 1966, provides infantry training up to platoon level, and advanced training to officers at company level, as well as specialised training in support weapons. There is also a school of artillery, a school of field engineers, and a technical training institute.

Before the British military withdrawal in 1971, naval and air cover was provided by the British, so that in building up the SAF the emphasis was laid initially on land forces. After the British decided to accelerate their withdrawal, it became necessary for Singapore to accelerate correspondingly the build-up of naval and air forces. The Maritime Command, officially formed as a regular unit of the SAF on 1 December 1968, relies largely on fast seaward defence patrol craft, of which it has six. The first of these 110ft patrol boats was launched in the United Kingdom in July 1969, but by November Singapore had itself built and launched the second. The patrol boats perform various duties in peacetime, including coastal patrol, air-sea rescue, and fisheries protection. Ratings are trained at the School of Maritime Training or at the Maritime Technical Training School, both of which have among their instructors some seconded from the Royal New Zealand Navy, and officer cadets are sent for training to Australia, Canada, New Zealand and the United Kingdom. The Ferry Transport Unit operates a fleet of harbour launches and landing craft which transport troops, vehicles and equipment to training areas on the offshore islands. The Maritime Command Boat Company operates a fleet of fast wooden Jarring boats powered by outboard motors. Coastal radar surveillance of territorial waters is carried out by the Radar Detection Unit.

From April 1968 a recruitment campaign was carried out to enlist volunteers for the Singapore Air Force Command. Recruits are sent to the Flying School at Seletar, and then go overseas for advanced training. The Singapore Air Defence Command now has a squadron of Hawker Hunters, a light aircraft squadron of Cessna-172s, a jet trainer squadron of BAC-167 Strikemasters, and a squadron of Alouette III helicopters. In 1971 it took over Bukit Gombak radar station, one of the most sophisticated radar shields in South East Asia, from the RAF. A Bloodhound surface-to-air missile system has been purchased from the British government, and assistance in operating it is being provided by the Australian government.

The SAF has an active combat strength of about 5,000, and all commands are assisted by volunteer bodies comprising the People's Defence Force (PDF), the Special Constabulary and the Vigilante Corps. The PDF was organised in 1966 with the volunteer corps of the former Singapore Military Forces as a nucleus. Like the regular forces, it is under the direct command of MINDEF. It is now organised into six infantry battalions, one engineers battalion and a PDF (Women) company. Its role is to release the regular troops for more difficult missions by guarding vital installations and manning road control points. The Vigilante Corps was formed in the wake of *konfrontasi* in 1964, to help the police carry out patrols against infiltrators, and continues to help with internal security patrols. Youth organisations not normally associated with military training agreed in 1971 to an education ministry 'suggestion' that they include rifle drill in their activities : weapon training is accordingly carried out by the Boy Scouts' and Girl Guides' Associations. and the Boys' and the Girls' Brigades.

INTERNATIONAL RELATIONS

The combined populations of Singapore's two nearest neighbours, Malaysia and Indonesia, total 120 million—sixty times that of Singapore itself. Both Malaysia and Indonesia have large communities of the Overseas Chinese, most of them acting as bankers, traders and shopkeepers, who have been settled there for two or more generations; and both Malaysia and Indonesia have been the scene of savage racial violence in the recent past. In Indonesia

141

there was a wholesale massacre of Chinese communists in 1965–6, and on 13 May 1969 terrifying racial strife broke out in the Malaysian capital, Kuala Lumpur. The cause of violence in each case rested in part on the resentment felt by the Malay peoples against the Chinese as non-Muslims; as the money-making entrepreneurs of the community; and as kin to, if not representatives of, the peoples of Communist China itself, the Asian giant with which the whole region must somehow come to a *modus vivendi* in the near future.

Singapore, mainly Chinese by population, entirely Malay in its location, and looking to western methods to help in its move to industrialisation, in some sense finds itself at the ellipse where three circles of influence overlap. To look to China as its mentor would be, apart from its inherent difficulties, to antagonise and badly frighten its huge Malay neighbours. To ally itself with the West in every respect, including culturally, is both impossible and distasteful to most of its people. To throw in its lot with Malaysia is a solution that has been tried, and found wanting.

Yet separation from Malaysia is as artificial, though in different respects, as was merger. The joint defence council established at separation has not as yet come to anything, since neither country is willing to depend on the other, but Singapore and Malaysia will have to co-operate on defence matters, if only to achieve such practical results as operating the radar network the British left behind; and a joint effort is needed to keep the Malayan Communist Party from having real influence. In economic and in personal terms, it is the same story. Singapore and Malaysia share a stock exchange, and their currencies, though separate, are freely interchangeable. Families are split between both sides of the Causeway, and indeed Lee Kuan Yew remarked in a speech made in 1969 that half his cabinet colleagues still have their families in West Malaysia.

Singapore thus has a very special, if difficult, regional relationship. Its position vis-à-vis Indonesia is as delicate as that regarding Malaysia, though based on a different colonial past. Indonesia,

142

with 110 million people, continues to depend a good deal on Singapore, by far the most 'advanced' country in the region, for the processing and marketing of her export commodities. About one-fifth of Indonesian foreign trade goes through the port of Singapore. The Singapore government is well aware of the dangers of resentment and envy as felt by one's neighbours, and Dr Goh Keng Swee has stated publicly that 'the successful take-off to self-sustaining industrial growth by our neighbours is the best guarantee of peace and stability in South East Asia'. Singapore encourages its businessmen to invest in Malaysian and Indonesian industrial projects, and gives them tax exemption on such investment.

Singapore is a founder member of the Association of South East Asian Nations (ASEAN), which was formed in 1967 with Indonesia, Malaysia, the Philippines and Thailand, and plays an active part in various regional organisations, including the United Nations Economic Commission for Asia and the Far East (ECAFE), and the Colombo Plan.

On the world stage, Singapore's chief concern, as a small nation largely dependent on foreign trade and ethnically distinct within its own region, is to cultivate friendly relations with as many countries as possible. Relationships with China and Taiwan present special difficulties since Singapore's population is, because of its ethnic and linguistic composition, particularly vulnerable to propaganda from both communists and Nationalists. There are no diplomatic relations with either Peking or Taiwan. Peking refuses to recognise independent Singapore, but Singapore allows the communists to deal through the Bank of China in Battery Road, and supported China's claim to a seat in the UN.

Another special relationship is that within the British Commonwealth: despite the British military withdrawal, Singapore's ties with Britain, Australia and New Zealand are very close, and all three have given her much military and economic support. The Five-Nation Commonwealth Defence Agreement, including also Malaysia, is expected to some extent to stop the gap left by the British withdrawal. The agreement was announced on 16 April 1971 after a meeting of defence ministers in London.

Feelings towards the USA are rather ambivalent. There are large numbers of American expatriates in Singapore, involved in industrial undertakings and the oil business, and the Singapore government, whilst greatly admiring American technological expertise, is less enthusiastic about the attitude of young Americans to authority, and deprecates most aspects of the permissive society. This ambivalence extends to the Vietnam war. Few Asians feel entirely happy about the way the Americans have handled it, yet if the whole of Indochina were to be given over to communism, with China as the chief communist power in the Far East, anti-Chinese feeling in the Malay peninsula and archipelago might well crystallise with terrible results for Singapore. There is little doubt that Singapore welcomes competition among the other great powers in the Far East : her official dealings with both Japan and Russia are cordial.

Relations between Japan and Singapore have softened, partly with the passing of time, partly because of the $50 million (£7·1 million; US $17 million) which was offered by the Japanese government as reparations for the massacre of civilians by Japanese soldiers during the occupation. Half of it took the form of loans on 'special terms', about which the respective governments are reticent, and part of the other $25 million was used as capital investment in Jurong Shipbuilders (Pte) Ltd, a partnership of the government, Jurong Shipyard, and a Japanese firm; part for the construction of the Sentosa earth satellite; and part for the purchase of equipment for such statutory bodies as the Public Utilities Board (PUB).

After only seven years of sovereign independence the republic's international relations are still developing. At the beginning of 1971 Singapore had sixteen resident diplomatic missions abroad, in Bangkok, Cairo, Canberra, Hong Kong, Jakarta, Kuala Lumpur, London, Manila, Moscow, New Delhi, New York, Phnompenh, Stockholm, Tokyo, Washington and Wellington.

There were twenty-three missions abroad in total, including those served from neighbouring capitals. These comprised seven high commissions (in Australia, Canada, Great Britain, India, Malaysia, New Zealand and Pakistan), twelve embassies (in Brazil, Cambodia, Ethiopia, Indonesia, Japan, Lebanon, Nepal, Philippines, Thailand, UAR, USA and Yugoslavia), a permanent mission at the United Nations in New York, a commission in Hong Kong, an honorary consulate in Sweden and a trade office in the Soviet Union. Accredited foreign diplomatic missions in Singapore at the same time numbered thirty-six, with an additional dozen or so consular offices. These represented all the countries mentioned above together with Argentina, Austria, Belgium, Bulgaria, Burma, Ceylon, Denmark, Finland, France, West Germany, Greece, Hungary, Israel, Italy, North Korea, Netherlands, Norway, Panama, Poland, Rumania, Saudi Arabia, Spain, Switzerland, Turkey and South Vietnam. Singapore was host to the thirty-one heads of government and other delegations at the Commonwealth Conference in January 1971, at which an impasse between the British and most African governments over arms sales was narrowly averted.

7   PUBLIC SERVICES

THE public services in Singapore have come a long way since the days of the notorious Captain Faber, who was appointed superintending engineer in 1844, and whom Buckley describes as the 'gallant officer who, on being told that he had built a bridge over the river so low that the *tongkangs* could not pass under it at high tide, had the bottom of the river dredged under the bridge to float them through'. Public works such as roadbuilding, sewerage and flood alleviation are now the responsibility of the Public Works Department (PWD) of the Ministry of Law and National Development. In recent years a good part of the annual budget has been allocated to works designed to prevent the occurrence of floods. Floods became a great nuisance, though seldom a risk to life, as a result of the destruction of vegetation and soil cover in the island's drainage basins during land clearance: Buckley relates, for example, of the great flood of 1892, that 'a gentleman had swam down Orchard Road with a three foot rule to gauge the depth; and the same day a gentleman canoed from Tanglin to the sea'.

There were four major floods between 1954 and 1970, but by 1961 the island had been made virtually flood-free except in the Bukit Timah area, where roads often became impassable. Drainage is now the most important consideration in all river development works, and some of Singapore's many small streams are being canalised, old drains are being renewed and widened, and concrete-lined canals are being built. The Bukit Timah Flood Alleviation scheme, on which work by the PWD began in 1967, is the first such scheme to use underground tunnels. Three stretches of twin tunnels, circular in shape and 12½–13½ft across in internal diameter, run under Malayan Railway lines and the Ulu Pandan Military Hill and beneath Garlick Avenue. The tunnels are supplemented by 8,143ft of open channel and 606ft of culvert.

The Public Utilities Board was established in 1963 as a statutory corporation to take over the functions of the former city council with regard to supplies of water, electricity and gas. It has obtained five loans from the World Bank, amounting to $225·9 million (£30·5 million; US $72·6 million) to finance its power generation, transmission and distribution network, and the development of water projects.

WATER

In the early years of the British settlement, wells were sunk along the base of Government Hill to supply both town and ships with water, and a small reservoir was constructed. In 1846, wells intended primarily for use in case of fire were sunk in Commercial Square and Malacca Street, and were covered with lids of planking laid flush to the road. Four others were constructed for public use in 1851 at the expense of Syed Ali Al-junied, who had noted 'the suffering of the poorer classes in particular, from the want of an adequate supply of good and wholesome water during the dry months'.

As Singapore's population and the numbers of ships using the harbour grew, the lack of a sufficient water supply became serious. In November 1857, a Chinese merchant, Tan Kim Seng, offered $13,000 (£1,750; US $4,330) for the construction of the means of a good supply in the town, but, after much discussion in high places, the money, though accepted, was frittered away and the only tangible result was a large fountain, put up to the memory of Tan Kim Seng's generosity by the municipality in 1882. Meantime, a series of droughts exacerbated matters, and in 1864 water was at times sold for five cents a bucket between

January and March. The supply to ships was at this time catered for partly by the enterprising firm of Hammer and Company, which plied its water boats between New Harbour, the Roads and a private reservoir on the island of Blakang Mati from 1863 onwards. Water had been ferried to ships from the government wells and aqueduct in the town by various private companies from the early days : in 1841, for example, five such companies were operating. The Tanjong Pagar Dock Company laid its own water mains in 1880.

Singapore remained without a proper water supply until 1878, when the municipal commissioners took over from the government what was left of the earlier waterworks, an impounding reservoir at Thomson Road which supplied the town by a stone conduit. The commissioners reconditioned the whole waterworks and replaced the conduit by a cast iron main. The first service reservoir was constructed on Mount Emily in the same year, when the first pumping station was installed, and the first filters, at Bukit Timah Road, were constructed about 1889, and later extended. A second service reservoir was constructed on Pearl's Hill in 1898. The Thomson Road reservoir, enlarged in 1891 and again in 1904, was the only source of water for the municipality until work on the Kallang river reservoir was begun in 1900. The Kallang river impounding reservoir was opened with new waterworks in 1911, together with the Woodleigh filter beds in Serangoon Road.

Modern Singapore's water supplies come both from within the republic itself and by pipeline across the Causeway from south Johore. There are three main impounding reservoirs, MacRitchie, Pierce and Seletar, in the 18 square miles of the catchment area. The Seletar reservoir, extended in 1969, increased its capacity from the 150 million gal it held when it was first constructed in 1940 to 5,300 million gal. At the same time, the capacity of the Woodleigh filter beds was expanded, to enable 54 million gal daily to be treated.

There were over 1,200 miles of main in use by 1970, and consumption continues to rise. The demand for water increased by 350 per cent between 1950 and 1970, and doubled between 1966 and 1971. In the early months of 1971, daily consumption reached 130 million gal, and dropped only after an intensive government campaign to save water, and a threat of water rationing.

GAS

For many years, lighting in Singapore was by means of coconut oil, though petroleum oil was used after 1868, and in certain places such as St Andrew's Cathedral candles were used to give dignity to the surroundings. The streets were first lit, by oil lamps, in 1824. Oil lighting gave way to gas for the first time on 24 May 1864, the date having been chosen to coincide with Queen Victoria's birthday, and Buckley describes how, when the lamps were first lit, 'natives were seen going up to the lamp-posts, and touching them very gingerly at first with the tips of their fingers; they could not understand how a fire could come out at the top, without the post getting hot'. He also noted that although 'the native shops and dwelling houses in town used gas pretty freely at first, it was replaced by oil in most instances in the course of time'. The Singapore Gas Co Ltd was a branch of a London company, and in 1901 its assets were purchased by the municipality. After this time, the use of gas for lighting increased, and profits were so good that the provision of electric lighting was perhaps longer delayed than it might otherwise have been.

Gas came into its own as a cooking fuel later in the century, and the number of gas consumers in Singapore increased from 42,782 in 1963 to 1,064,210 in 1970. There are six production units at the Kallang Gas Works, and in July 1970 a new Vickers-Zimmer gas-manufacturing plant was commissioned. This increased gas-making capacity by 36 per cent, from 315 million units to 430 million units per annum. Liquefied gas is widely used in Singapore outside the existing pipeline distribution system.

SINGAPORE

ELECTRICITY

Electricity was installed in the workshops of the Tanjong Pagar Dock Company before the end of the nineteenth century, in order to double the possible number of working hours, but Singapore streets were first lit by electricity only on 6 March 1906, and even in 1919 electric lighting was still rare outside the town centre. Electric power was purchased in bulk from the Singapore Electric Tramway Co, and sold by the municipality for distribution as a monopoly.

Today, the annual per capita consumption of electricity is one of the highest in the region, and amounts to about 820kW hours. The generation of electricity has been increasing consistently since 1963 at an average rate of 15 per cent per annum, and by 1970 about 2,000 million units were generated yearly. The PUB has three power stations: St James (49mW); Pasir Panjang 'A' (175mW) and 'B' (240mW), and these, together with the four 60mW units put into use at the Jurong Power Station in 1970, give a total installed generating capacity of 704mW. Four more 60mW units are to be installed at Jurong by 1973, and ultimately the generating power of the station is to be increased to 600mW, owing to the demands for power from large industries in this industrial town. Submarine cables have been laid from Jurong Power Station to the oil refineries on Pulau Ayer Chawan, Pulau Merlimau and Pulau Bukom, and the installation is one of the largest 66kV submarine cable systems in the world.

Over 880 miles of highways, roads, tracks and villages had public street lighting by 1970, and the total number of substations commissioned was 1,178, most of them intended to supply power for commerce and industry. Singapore was the first state in Asia to introduce the new sulphur-hexafluoride (SF6) insulated small oil volume 66kV metal-clad switchgear; this was used at the 66/22/6·6kV substation commissioned at Crawford Street in 1969 under the Urban Renewal Plan. In 1971, the Asian

150

Development Bank granted the PUB a loan of $46·41 million
(£6·63 million; US $15·47 million), for the expansion of Singa-
pore's power and distribution system. The loan will be used to
finance the foreign exchange cost of the supply and installation of
lines for a 230kV transmission.

FIRES AND FIRE SERVICES

Many large-scale fires broke out in Singapore's early years, made
worse by the fact that building was at first unrestricted and that
there was no properly organised protection : such a fire, in 1822,
bankrupted Naraina Pillai, the foremost among Singapore's
Indian merchants. Another, in 1830, burned down Philip Street
and one side of Market Street, and raged for three days and
nights. Bands of convicts, soldiers and volunteers, handling
buckets of water, strove to put it out.

There were many more fires in the next fifteen years, and by
1846, as a result of popular agitation, the police had acquired a
fire engine, though a ready supply of water was seldom available.
By 1864 the police had two manually operated engines, the firm
of Guthrie and Co had one, and the convicts had one at the jail,
but the efforts of all together availed little when the first fire ever
known in the European quarter of the town broke out, on New
Year's Eve. A ship's chandler's store at the corner of Battery
Road and Flint Street was burned out and the fire spread to
adjacent buildings. Boat crews landed from ships in the harbour,
and soldiers came down from Fort Canning, but all had to be
removed by their officers when they began to help themselves to
the bottles of liquor revealed by the fire.

The first properly equipped professional fire brigade was
formed in 1888, and the number of fires soon decreased, perhaps
because the brigade's efficiency made it less desirable to set fires
in the hope of claiming insurance. Eight years later, the traditional practice of signalling an outbreak by firing a gun from Fort
Canning was dropped, and in 1915 a system of street fire alarms

151

was established. Singapore's fire engines were horse-drawn until 1912.

Today there are five fire stations in Singapore, including the Central Fire Station in Hill Street, and there are thirty-six engines in use. The brigade responds to about two thousand calls annually. An Auxiliary Fire Service was formed early in 1972 from national servicemen deployed from the Vigilante Corps. In 1970, 3,823 fire prevention inspections were carried out within the port and at the Keppel dockyard and Jurong shipyard by the PSA Fire Brigade, and in 1969 a special unit was formed to combat sea pollution within the inner harbour of the port. In its first year, the unit recovered 73 tons of flotsam and used 4,907 gal of detergent in dispersing oil slicks.

In modern times, as in earlier days, many of Singapore's largest fires were probably caused by fireworks set off at Chinese New Year : this was true of two fires in 1968, one of which destroyed the Ellenborough market, the other consuming 22 stalls at the Gay World Amusement Park. The most disastrous of recent fires, however, occurred long after Chinese New Year, on 25 May 1961. It broke out at about 3.30pm in Tiong Bahru, and swept across to Bukit Ho Swee and on to Havelock Road, fanned by a strong wind, before burning out in the Delta Circus area : it was brought under control late the same night. Two hundred and fifty acres, covered by blocks of shophouses, oil mills, timber yards and engineering workshops, were devastated, and hundreds of crowded *attap* houses destroyed. Sixteen thousand people were made homeless, though only four persons were killed and 85 injured. The cost of the fire was estimated at $2·5 million (£357,140; US $833,330). Its cause is not known. Since the Bukit Ho Swee fire, particular stress has been laid on fire prevention in the work of the Fire Brigade.

8   TRADE AND INDUSTRY

WITH no natural resources other than its location, its harbour and the brains and energy of its colonisers and immigrant workers, Singapore had become, by 1900, the world's seventh busiest port. Its prosperity was founded on the *entrepôt* trade, and this state of affairs continued until well after World War II. Then problems arose : Singapore's trade and commerce were affected by *konfrontasi* and by the separation from Malaysia. *Entrepôt* trade is particularly sensitive to political and economic changes in the countries of trading partners, and Singapore has no raw materials of her own to fall back on. The British withdrawal meant a loss of earnings from abroad, as well as unemployment for an estimated 25,000 base technicians and auxiliary workers. These facts, together with the growth of the population, made it essential for the government to broaden Singapore's economic base.

In 1961 a UN Industrial Survey team advised Singapore to launch a crash industrial programme to provide at least 10,000 more jobs annually. Since then, the PAP government has done everything in its power to industrialise Singapore's economy, to attract investment, promote exports and find new markets. Its success so far is impressive.

The Gross Domestic Product at factor-cost grew from $1,968 million (£266 million; US $656 million) in 1959 to $5,565 million (£750 million; US $1,855 million) in 1970; the average annual increase between 1968–70 was almost 15 per cent. In 1960 there were 220 factories of ten or more employees. There are now more than 1,750. The value of manufacturing output rose from $399 million (£54 million; US $133 million) in 1959 to $3,983 million (£538 million; US $1,328 million) in 1970, and the gross value added in industry from $143 million (£19 million; US $48 million) to $1,154 million (£156 million; US $385 million). Whilst the population rose by about 25 per cent, from 1,580,000 to 2,070,000, between 1959 and 1970, government revenue rose from $275 million (£37 million; US $92 million) to $1,169 million (£158 million; US $390 million). Singapore thus surpassed the UN target of a 5-per-cent annual growth for the Development Decade of the sixties. The per capita income, $2,682 (£362·4; US $894) in 1970, is the highest in South East Asia and the highest in Asia after Japan.

The causes of this successful expansion of the economy have been, besides the development of industry as distinct from trade, Singapore's growth as an international banking centre, the increase in foreign investment, the improvement in the standard of the population's technological skills, and the development of maritime interests in shipping, and in submarine oil exploration.

Singapore has thus made considerable advances in the task of changing from an *entrepôt* trade economy to an *entrepôt* manufacturing economy. From her days as a colony she inherited a useful infrastructure of well-developed public utilities and communications, but these have been very considerably improved on since independence, and investment has been encouraged by the growth of banking and insurance facilities, by the reliability of the currency, and by the stability of the government and its relations with labour. Apart from £50 million (US $125 million) in grants and credits given by the British at the time of their withdrawal, and some World Bank and ADB loans for specific projects, Singapore has advanced very much under her own steam, without benefit of foreign aid.

Despite the change of balance from trade to industry, the port continues to be of prime importance to Singapore's economy.

Page 155 Yesterday and today: *(above)* junks lying in the Roads, from an oil painting by J. T. Thomson, about 1850. Government Hill and the first Anglican Cathedral are in the background; *(below)* the Causeway, the only one in the world joining two sovereign states

Page 156 Edwardian transport: *(above)* horse and carriage, 1903; *(below)* Esplanade and Padang, 1905–10, from a painting by A. L. Watson, showing cars, carriages, gharries and rickshaws

History

The advantages of Singapore's sheltered, deep-water harbour, navigable throughout the year, proved greater than Raffles realised. In the early years of the British settlement, ships anchored on the waterfront opposite the Singapore river, and their cargoes were carried by lighters direct to the godowns on Boat Quay. Keppel Harbour, further west and now the site of the Port of Singapore Authority's main installations, had been used by the Portuguese in the sixteenth century, but it fell into disuse and was not discovered by the British until August 1819. Even then, its entrance being too narrow for square-rigged ships, it was not used much until the advent of steam traffic and the establishment of the P & O service between Bombay, Singapore and Hong Kong. At this time it was known as New Harbour : its name was changed in 1900.

In 1848 Captain (later Admiral Sir) Henry Keppel discovered deep water close to the shore, 'among the numerous prettily wooded islands on the westward entrance to the Singapore river', had it surveyed, and suggested it as a site for a coaling station. In 1852 the P & O Company established a wharf and coaling station on Tebing Tinggi, a headland to the north of New Harbour. Other firms followed.

From the 1840s various proposals to build a dry dock were made, but it was not until 1859 that William Cloughton, a former merchant captain, built Singapore's first, to the west of the P & O Company's property. In 1864 the Tanjon Pagar Dock Company (TPDC) was registered, and opened its first dry dock, the Victoria, in October 1868. The company's first line of wharves, completed at Tanjong Pagar in 1866, was 750ft long and could berth four ships of average size. The wharves were extremely well situated, being very near to the eastern entrance to New Harbour, and only one mile from the godowns of the town square, to which cargo was carried by the company's bullock carts for transhipment by coastal steamers.

Singapore $ Million

	1959	1960	1961	1962	1963	1964	1965	1966	1967	1968	1969	1970
Agriculture and fishing	121·0	124·0	135·0	138·0	146·8	142·0	139·6	152·8	146·0	148·2	154·2	162·2
Manufacturing* (excluding rubber processing and quarrying)	170·2	187·4	218·3	246·8	294·8	330·5	414·3	486·8	616·5	716·0	897·2	1,153·5
Construction	40·3	41·9	66·0	71·0	94·7	113·9	130·6	128·7	150·1	179·8	212·9	290·4
Electricity, gas and water services	45·5	47·3	47·2	53·0	52·8	59·2	54·0	73·3	92·7	108·8	119·5	136·0
Wholesale and retail trade	624·0	630·1	703·9	717·8	859·4	708·1	772·0	878·7	998·5	1,308·6	1,547·9	1,695·0
Entrepôt trade*	(370·0)	(381·1)	(388·9)	(378·8)	(441·1)	(286·2)	(307·8)	(349·0)	(408·5)	(538·7)	(666·1)	(636·0)
Domestic trade	(254·0)	(269·0)	(315·0)	(339·0)	(418·3)	(421·9)	(464·2)	(529·7)	(589·6)	(769·9)	(881·8)	(1,059·0)
Ownership of dwellings	84·6	92·6	101·0	104·0	110·4	118·1	128·7	141·5	152·5	167·2	184·6	206·9
Government services	110·4	106·6	144·0	164·0	189·0	191·0	214·3	246·4	264·9	300·3	321·0	393·6
Other services	772·0	796·1	824·4	876·8	935·9	1,037·5	1,189·9	1,257·0	1,270·9	1,328·1	1,402·8	1,526·9
Military services	(271·0)	(279·0)	(280·9)	(301·0)	(323·0)	(412·4)	(519·1)	(549·5)	(489·9)	(456·9)	(404·1)	(405·4)
Tourism	(42·0)	(30·5)	(31·6)	(40·3)	(54·5)	(60·6)	(64·5)	(83·4)	(121·7)	(145·3)	(225·1)	(272·4)
Other*	(459·0)	(486·6)	(511·9)	(535·5)	(558·4)	(564·5)	(606·3)	(624·1)	(659·3)	(725·9)	(773·6)	(849·1)
Gross Domestic Product at Factor Cost	1,968·0	2,046·0	2,239·8	2,371·4	2,683·8	2,700·3	3,043·4	3,365·2	3,692·1	4,257·0	4,840·1	5,564·5

* Revision due to reclassification of processing items and SHB dockyard repairing services.

NB: £1 = Singapore $7·4
US $1 = Singapore $3·0

GROSS DOMESTIC PRODUCT
1959–70

The opening of the Suez Canal and the coming of the telegraph led to an extraordinary increase in steamship trade, and a consequent expansion in the dock facilities required. By 1870 there were four graving docks in New Harbour, plus the wharves of the TPDC and several other companies on the north side, and bunkering piers on the south side. In 1870 the TPDC declared a profit of $22,736 (£3,070; US $7,575) and in 1879 opened the Albert Dock to the east of the Victoria Dock. The company's wharves attracted the larger ships with bulky and valuable cargo such as machinery. From 1885 onwards, the TPDC began buying out its rivals and in 1899, after amalgamation with the New Harbour Dock Co, it held a virtual monopoly. The rapid increase in the size of European navies in the 1890s, coupled with the sharp rise in world trade, made its efficiency a matter of public concern. On 1 July 1905 the TPDC was taken over by the government, and in 1906 a Harbour Board was established in its stead. This unfortunately led to a division of control in the port, since whilst the docks were put under the administration of the Harbour Board, the control of shipping lying in the roadstead between the eastern and western anchorages continued to be the responsibility of the Master Attendant.

The Master Attendant was one of the first posts established in 1819, and for many years the captain of every ship in port had to seek his permission to land cargo or leave port, and must furnish him with details of all passengers. The Master Attendant was also responsible for the maintenance of signal stations and all aids to navigation.

In 1957 the control of navigational aids passed to the Light Dues Board, composed of representatives of users of the port and representatives of the government, with the Master Attendant as chairman. The services involved continued to be carried out by the Marine Department. At the end of 1963, the Master Attendant's title was changed to Director of Marine, and on 1 May 1964 the control of the port and all functions connected with its operation were transferred to the Port of Singapore Authority

(PSA), which was established as a statutory board. On 1 November 1971, the PSA took over from the British Far East Command the responsibility for all Singapore territorial waters within the Straits of Johore, thus almost doubling the area under its authority.

The Modern Port

Singapore is now the fourth busiest port in the world, in terms of gross tonnage of shipping cleared, after Rotterdam, New York and Yokohama, and the first in the British Commonwealth. It is an important bunkering port and one of the largest oil refining, blending and distribution centres in the world. During the 1960s it showed an average annual increase of 10 per cent in the cargo handled, and of $7\frac{1}{2}$ per cent in the tonnage of ships cleared. In 1950 a total of 10,963 vessels with a net registered tonnage of 29·1 million tons entered and cleared the port; by 1970 the number of vessels was 38,066 with a net registered tonnage of 148·7 million tons. The increase in total cargo handled over the same period rose from 6·2 million freight tons to 42·1 million freight tons. Of this, in 1970 82·9 per cent was handled in the Roads, and 17·1 per cent at the wharves.

The PSA manages, operates and develops the port and employs about 12,000 workers. The area it administers (excluding territorial waters in the Straits of Johore) covers about 125 square miles of water, plus a land area of about 950 acres, including 3 miles of wharves, 16 miles of metre gauge railway track connected with the main Malayan railway system, and an internal road system of about 12 miles. The wharves accommodate thirty vessels at a time, and all twenty-five berths for oceangoing ships and five berths for coasters are serviced by transit sheds, forklift trucks and mobile cranes, diesel and fuel oil bunkers, and fresh water. The PSA has at its disposal 2·5 million sq ft of covered storage space, and cargo handling and berthing and unberthing services continue all round the clock. Within the port area, six oil refineries and two oil installations supply oil to all ships. A total

160

of seventeen marine terminal berths are owned and operated by five of the world's largest oil companies, three of which have begun major refinery expansion programmes.

The deep-water berths extend from Keppel Harbour to Tanjong Pagar, and in the adjoining Telok Ayer area to the east are the coastal wharves and lighterage basin for shallow-draft vessels of up to 14ft. The basin is used for unloading cargoes coming from China, Taiwan and Hong Kong. The East Lagoon Container Complex, completed ahead of schedule late in 1971, already operates a 700ft cross-berth for container feeder services, and includes 2,250ft of marginal wharves for container ships, a diaphragm breakwater of about 250ft for protection during the monsoon period, and a back-up area of about a hundred acres. Shore-based container cranes have been installed along the container berths to deal with ships whose average size is 60,000 tons.

The Eastern and Western Roads provide unlimited anchorage for vessels of any draft. The Western Roads are used by ocean shipping and the Eastern Roads are divided into the Outer and Inner Roads by a mole constructed in 1907, half a mile from the entrance to the Singapore river. The PSA also controls the Singapore, Rochore and Kallang rivers as far as they are navigable, and has berthing facilities on the islands of Pulau Sebarok, Tanjong Penjuru and Pulau Bukom.

Ship-building and ship-repairing

Singapore has about fifty shipyards, although less than a third of these can build ships of the class of 1,500–2,000 tons, and only one can build up to 5,000 tons. The Keppel shipyard, formerly under the control of the PSA, and Sembawang, the former British naval base dockyard, are government-owned, and some of the other shipyards are partly owned by the government.

Shipyard output doubled from 1966 to 1968, producing ships to the value of £18 million (US $43·2 million) in 1968. Jurong shipyard has begun to build 'Freedom' freighters of 15,000dwt

161

tons, as well as a variety of smaller craft and specialised vessels. With the expansion of offshore oil prospecting, begun in 1960, Singapore has begun the construction and assembly of oil rigs and auxiliary equipment.

The government plans to make Singapore the largest ship-repairing and ship-building centre east of Suez and south of Japan. The hub of commercial ship repairs will be the Sembawang dockyard, the conversion of which from a British naval base to a Singapore-owned commercial establishment was phased to coincide with the stages of the British withdrawal. There are three dry docks for ships of 90–100,000dwt tons, one of which is capable of being extended to 300,000dwt tons. Much depends on whether a sufficient supply of skilled labour and of engineers and supervisors can be maintained and developed.

TRADE

Singapore's *entrepôt* trade, which used very recently to be about equal as a component of the Gross National Product with manufacturing industry, is declining : it currently amounts to about one-tenth. Rubber, which accounts for 20 per cent of Singapore's total trade, is the largest single item; petroleum and petroleum products come second. Singapore is the oil products storage and distribution centre for the whole region, and the Shell oil refinery on Pulau Bukom is the largest in Asia and the fourth largest in the world. Textiles are a third important trading commodity.

Singapore continues to bring in its traditional imports of rubber, tin, rattan, copra, palm oil, timber, coffee, pepper, rice and spices from nearby countries for re-export. Today, however, the emphasis is moving rapidly from trade in raw materials to trade in Singapore's own manufactures. Imported raw materials are graded, milled, re-packed and processed in various ways, before re-export, but in addition there have been import substitutions of such commodities as sugar, petroleum, cigarettes, beer, stout, condensed milk, paint and cement, which are replaced by products made locally.

Singapore's chief trading partner is Japan, followed by West Malaysia, Indonesia, the USA, UK, China, Australia and Sarawak. Trade with the USSR and the countries of Eastern Europe is increasing, largely as a result of the efforts of Intraco. Intraco is one of a number of government-inspired institutions intended to stimulate Singapore's trade and industry. Incorporated in November 1968 as an international trading company, it is 30 per cent government-owned and 70 per cent privately-owned, but run by the civil service. It was set up to deal with the state trading organisations of socialist countries, but it also seeks wide markets for local manufactures, and trades, through its overseas offices, with thirty countries including some in Africa. It organises bulk buying and selling of raw materials for local industry, and has investments in banks, insurance, container, warehousing, transportation, logging and various industries manufacturing products such as wigs, flour, shoes, garments, textiles, and vegetable oil.

Both the Jurong port and the area within the PSA perimeter fence were, from September 1969, declared free trade zones for the transhipment and re-export of goods to neighbouring countries. A curious feature of Singapore's trade is the official recognition of barter, which survives from Singapore's earliest days, and which mainly concerns trade with Indonesia. A barter trade control area of six acres, with storage sheds, offices, overnight living quarters and supplies of food and drink has been set up at Pasir Panjang.

BANKING AND INDUSTRY

Singapore at independence inherited two banking systems : the British, including representatives of foreign banks, and the local banks, which had grown prosperous from the 1930s onwards, and which had set up a local money and capital market in order to make Singapore independent of the London market. Of the 37 banks operating in Singapore in 1971, 11 were incorporated in Singapore, 4 in Malaysia, and the rest were from Britain, India, America, Hong Kong, China, Japan, France, Holland, Thailand and Indonesia. Credit institutions include finance companies, mainly concerned with hire-purchase and mortgages, a few building societies, and scores of co-operative thrift societies, the members of which are mainly government employees considered a good financial risk. The earliest group of moneylenders, the *chettiars*, survive, but charge extremely high rates of interest.

In November 1968 the government opened the first Asian Dollar Market for offshore US dollar accounts, and in April 1969 established the Singapore Gold Market for the import of gold for sale to non-residents; the gold market already surpasses in importance that of Hong Kong. The additional facility of secret numbered accounts was introduced in 1970. Singapore's currency is one of the most stable in the world, and its gold and foreign exchange reserves exceed US $800 million (£333 million).

In the drive to develop the industrial side of the economy which began in the 1960s, the government took measures to stimulate long term credit for capital investment purposes on a scale hitherto eschewed by the local banks. Thus, it set up in 1968 the Development Bank of Singapore (DBS) to provide financial assistance for the development of industry in the form of medium and long term loans, equity participation, and guarantees to manufacturing, processing, service and other industries. The DBS aims to offer assistance to projects it considers technically and economically sound where local commercial banks are unable or unwilling to risk large sums. The bank, which borrowed $30 million (£4 million; US $10 million) for a fourteen-year term from the Asian Development Bank in 1969, is 51-per-cent privately owned, the rest of the shares belonging to the government. It has investments in hotels, electronics, wood products and petroleum, and by 1970 75 per cent of its assistance had been given to fifty-two joint ventures with, and twelve wholly-owned subsidiaries of, foreign companies.

Government participation in commercial enterprises is considerable, and has often called forth criticism and signs of disquiet from the private sector, which fears unfair competition. The PAP government's main intention, however, seems to be to stimulate private enterprise, to fulfil industrial needs and accept industrial challenges, though there is no doubt that it also wishes to keep certain services vital to Singapore's economy partly within its own control. Examples of these separate ambitions may be seen in the fact that the government has invested heavily in the tourist hotel industry, and that it owns Singapore's share of Malaysia-Singapore Airlines, the local shipping line, Neptune Orient, the National Iron and Steel Mills, and the two largest shipyards. It also has equity holdings in twenty-one industrial banking and communications companies.

In 1961, as part of its programme to help rapid industrialisation, the government set up the Economic Development Board (EDB). Originally, it was the means by which investment opportunities were sought out, and industrial projects evaluated and implemented. With its various specialised divisions, including technical consultant services and economic research groups, it had the responsibility of developing industrial estates and ensuring the success of new projects as far as possible. The EDB's work was thus to smooth the way at every stage from the provision of the necessary finance through the administrative formalities to the acquisition of factory accommodation, with all attendant services such as power, water, and transport. Subsequently the DBS took over the EDB's financial functions, and the control and development of industrial estates was passed to the Jurong Town Corporation (JTC), formed on 1 June 1968.

Jurong

The development of Jurong, Singapore's great industrial estate, has been one of the most remarkable feats in Singapore's modern history. It was the brainchild of Dr Goh Keng Swee and was at first christened 'Goh's Folly' by some sceptical observers. From 1961, $100 million (£13·6 million; US $33·3 million) of public money was put into the task of draining the Jurong swamp, in the south-west corner of the island, and turning it into a vast industrial estate which would eventually become a town. The site was considered ideal because of its size, the fact that it would entail no resettlement problem, and the possibility of building a port usefully near to Singapore's main port and the routes of the great oil tankers. Once the land was prepared, the EDB supervised the provision of electric power, water, sewerage, roads, railways and houses, and built wharves. It then proceeded to build and rent out or sell fully serviced factories. By 1971, Jurong had 317 factories in production, and plans had been made for about eighty-four more; 5,553 acres were already fully developed, with over a thousand further acres under development. The town is served by a 3,000ft deep-water wharf and 1,260ft of coastal and lighter wharves (which became busy enough to be officially renamed Jurong Port in 1970), 12 miles of railway linking it with the main Singapore-Malaysian line, 27 miles of metalled roads, a 48in diameter water main, capable of supplying 30 million gal of fresh water per day, and an industrial plant capable of supplying 10 million gal of high quality industrial water. Jurong, which is Singapore's main bulk-handling port, deals with over one million tons of cargo annually, and over a thousand vessels call there each year. It is administered by the PSA.

Goods manufactured in Jurong include metal products, heavy transport equipment, petroleum, building materials, electrical parts, chemicals and pharmaceuticals, rubber and leather, pulp and paper, textiles and garments, and food products. By 1970 Jurong's factories employed some 36,000 workers, and with the provision of housing, bus services to other parts of the island, parks and a hospital, the industrial estate had blossomed into a town. All this had risen within the space of a decade, from an uninhabited waste of swampland. On its completion in 1975

Jurong town will cover 12,000 acres, or 18·75 square miles, and have 70,000 workers.

The JTC was established to develop and manage all industrial estates and sites in Singapore, and to provide amenities for the people living there. It controls a number of smaller industrial estates, with an aggregate total of about 200 factories. One such site, at Kranji, covers 750 acres and has made possible the centralisation of sawmills and timber firms and the control of pollution arising from the wood industry.

New Industries

In addition to the establishment of the EDB and the DBS, and increasing emphasis on the technological side of education, the Singapore government encouraged industrial growth during the 1960s by giving certain tax exemptions to firms establishing pioneer industries new to Singapore. These exemptions have been pared down with growing industrialisation, and the government is now much more selective in granting privileges. By 1969 there were 236 pioneer industries established, employing 35,000 workers and producing goods to the value of $1,226 million (£165 million; US $409 million) — 44 per cent of the total value of manufactures. In the early 1960s, with the prospect of 25,000 school leavers annually seeking jobs by the end of the decade, it was the labour intensive industries, such as textiles, which were sought after. A few years later, Singapore, as a result of industrial growth plus the effect of compulsory national service, drew near to full employment, and the result was a switch to capital intensive and high-technology industry.

Between 1965 and 1970, industrial output more than doubled. In 1960 only 10 per cent of the Gross National Product was contributed by the manufacturing sector, but by 1970 this had risen to 20 per cent, and industry now surpasses *entrepôt* trading in contributing to national employment. Major industrial groups showing significant increase in production by the late 1960s included petroleum refining, shipbuilding and repairing, the manu-

167

facture of wearing apparel and made-up textile goods, chemicals and chemical products, wood and cork, and electrical goods and appliances.

Singapore is now the largest petroleum refining, blending and distributing centre in South East Asia. By 1971 its refining capacity was 370,000 barrels per day, and by 1973 this is expected to rise to over half a million. Products include base lubricants and solvents. Of the US $50 million (£20·9 million) invested by the USA in Singapore, 40 per cent is taken up by petroleum and chemical products. The electronics industry came into being about the end of 1968, and various types of electronic components are manufactured, such as transistors, diodes, integrated circuits, capacitors, resistors, and rotary and magnetic components, as well as transistor radio and TV sets.

The government has particularly encouraged the growth of the metal fabrication industry. There has been a great expansion of foundries and forging operations. Intensive efforts have also been made to develop precision engineering, especially in the making of tools, dies, jigs and fixtures, gauges and measuring instruments, optical instruments, and watches. Several internationally famous firms, including Plessey and Beecham of Britain, Philips of Holland, Siemens and Rolleiwerke of Germany, and General Electric of the USA, have invested in very substantial factories, some of which are responsible for making production equipment to serve the company's head office and subsidiaries throughout the world. The trend is therefore towards industries requiring high technological skills. The total cumulative figure of private foreign investment in manufacturing industry reached almost US $340 million (£113 million) by 1971 —over one-third of it from the US, one-fifth from Britain, and one-sixth from Holland. In 1970, more than half of new investment was American, and this trend continued into 1971. Only 7 per cent came from Japan, and 5 per cent from Hong Kong.

In line with this effort towards greater industrial sophistication is the start that has recently been made in the establishment of an aerospace industry. In 1969 the former RAF Seletar airfield and base were taken over to provide facilities for the Singapore General Aviation Service, a joint venture between the Singapore government and Hawker de Havilland.

Official encouragement of large-scale industry and foreign investment has not always been understood or fully accepted by the hundreds of workers, mostly Chinese, running tiny one-family factories manufacturing various goods made of metal, wood or rattan, in Chinatown or the suburbs. Like the farmers and the *kampong* dwellers compulsorily moved from their homes to provide space for housing or industrial projects, some feel that they are being hurled from their traditional way of life into the modern world without consideration.

Labour

The comparative stability of labour's relations with government and industry has been of great importance in attracting foreign investment. Trade unionism began in 1946, when the British allowed registration, and it quickly became communist-controlled. The 1950s were bedevilled by constant strikes, and in 1961 there was a total loss of 410,891 man days. In that year came the split between the left and right wings of the PAP, and when the left wing had been expelled, later to form the Barisan Sosialis, the PAP began the task of organising its own unions. It came to power largely on their backs. From the mid-1960s the government exercised stringent control, and the result of its tactics is that labour relations are governed by what has been described as a 'blend of free collective bargaining with compulsory arbitration'.

There are only two Trade Union Federations in Singapore: the National Trades Union Council (NTUC) and the loose grouping formed by the rest. Seventy-three per cent of members of the 106 employees' unions registered belonged, by 1970, to the thirty-nine unions affiliated to the NTUC (there are fifty-three employers' unions). Seven unions of the Singapore Association of

Trade Unions (SATU), originally a rival leftwing body, had their registrations cancelled in 1964 because of a government charge that they were involved in a communist plot to create disorder.

Strikes in the public utilities are illegal, and both strikes and lockouts are prohibited whilst a case is pending before the industrial arbitration courts, of which there are two. Most cases are heard by three members: one from the employer's panel, one from the employees' panel, and the president or deputy-president acting as chairman. No appeal against the awards of the court is permitted. The Labour Research Unit, which is partly financed by the government, seconds its officers to assist trade unions in the preparation of claims and their presentation before the court. The finances of the trade unions are to some extent dependent on the generosity of the government, and government influence, at least on broad policy questions, is strong. Membership of unions is high in the public sector, but elsewhere there is a good deal of apathy, membership being mostly in the larger and foreign-directed firms in the manufacturing, petroleum and service industries. Only one-third of the total labour force is unionised, and loss of man days through industrial disputes is now negligible.

There is no guaranteed minimum wage. The average monthly wage in 1970 was $270 (£36; US $90). In general a 44-hour week is worked, with one rest day, and eleven paid holidays a year, plus 7–14 days' annual leave, depending on length of service. Despite the advance of technological education, necessary skills remain in short supply, and in 1970 the government put forward a scheme to attract immigrants with special technical and managerial skills, promising them citizenship. Between 1959 and 1969, productive employment in manufacturing industries rose from 25,199 to 106,838.

TOURISM

Singapore's international tourist trade is rising by over 20 per cent yearly, and in 1970 more than 540,000 visitors arrived by air or sea, excluding those coming in over the Causeway from Malaysia. By the end of 1971, 11,308 hotel rooms were available, a vast hotel building programme having taken place over the previous few years. Singapore has done much to attract the tourist trade, beginning with the campaign against professional beggars in 1964, and rising to a peak in the seventies with the development of the island of Sentosa specifically as a tourist resort. In 1970 the largest percentage of visitors were Americans, followed by Britons, Indonesians, Australians and Malaysians. By 1970, earnings from the tourist industry had reached $272 million (£36 million; US $91 million) annually.

Nevertheless, Singapore has less to offer the tourist than many countries in the Far East. The publicity slogan 'Instant Asia' perhaps suggests its deficiencies as well as its attractions. The variety of races living harmoniously and practising their own customs, the luxury and efficiency of the hotels, and the cleanliness of the streets certainly have an appeal. On the other hand, Singapore is without spectacular natural scenery, a large proportion of its citizens wear western dress, and in the central business districts and the Orchard Road area favoured by the big hotels there is little except climate to differentiate Singapore from the cities of Europe and the United States. Most buildings with an indigenous style of architecture are being swept away : the changes which come in the wake of industrialisation carry away with them the picturesque features of life which appeal to tourists. Singapore's greatest advantages for tourists are perhaps the prevalence of English as the language of shops, hotels and many of the ordinary citizens, and its convenience as a jumping-off place for visits to Malaysia and Indonesia, a fact recognised by the Singapore government's investment in the Bali hotel industry.

The Tourist Promotion Board was set up in 1964 as a government agency, and receives $500,000 (£68,000; US $160,500) annually from the government, plus a 3-per-cent cess levied on hotels and restaurants of a certain standard. Tourists are allowed in without visas for a seven-day visit, but only if they are in possession of 'ample funds' and can produce firm bookings onwards, or return tickets. This is a way of sifting out hippies, from whose supposed contamination the government has shown itself very eager to protect Singapore, not merely objecting to drug-taking, but also conducting a vigorous campaign against long hair for men. Nationals from communist countries or Taiwan must always apply for a visa.

Page 173 Dock facilities: *(above)* waterfront, showing the Telok Ayer Basin and part of the Inner Roads; *(below)* aerial view of the dry docks of the Port of Singapore Authority

Page 174 The new Singapore: *(above)* aerial view of Jurong Port; *(below)* Jurong town and industrial estate under construction

9 AGRICULTURE AND FISHERIES

AGRICULTURE has never been of great importance to the economy, but has become even less so in recent years, and, with land so short, other uses take priority. Full-time farmers are re-settled by the government if their land is taken for industry or housing, but no land is granted to part-time farmers so moved, and in 1971 the MP for Chua Chu Kang, Mr Tang See Chim, told farmers that the government considers vegetable farming a waste of land and human resources, and urged them to prepare to change their way of life. Agriculture and fisheries together constitute less than 3 per cent of Singapore's economic activity. About fifty-five square miles or 24·5 per cent of the total land area is under cultivation, and in 1970 there were 20,357 licensed farms, most of them family concerns of between 2 and 2½ acres, but some of them as small as a quarter of an acre. Many of their owners are descendants of those nineteenth-century Chinese who farmed vegetables along the valleys where there was a high water content. Today, about 41,000 tons of vegetables annually are grown, amounting to over half the island's total requirements. Vegetables include choy san (*brassica rapa*), pak choy (*brassica chinensis*), Chinese kale (*brassica alboglabra*), lettuce, watercress, celery, cucumber, hairy gourd, bitter gourd, long bean, brinjal, chilli and radish. Vegetables are farmed in rotation with tobacco in the west and north of the island, and there are market gardens in the Ama Keng agricultural settlement. About 6,300 acres are under fruit cultivation. Local fruits include the rambutan, durian, banana, papaya, starfruit (*averrhoa carambola*), mango, lemon, nangka (*artocarpus heterophyllus*), and jambu (*psidium guajava*).

SINGAPORE

Livestock

The tradition in family plots is of mixed farming, but the government, through the department of primary production under the Ministry of National Development, encourages the trend towards specialisation. Poultry and pig farming are of importance, since they provide the main meats consumed in Singapore, and the Pig and Poultry Research Training Institute was set up in 1968 with the help of the UN Development Programme Special Fund. A veterinary research station at Sembawang and the ten veterinary extension centres scattered throughout the island, together with seventy-two rural community centres, advise on farming management and techniques, and assist in the production of good breeds of pigs and poultry to improve the farmers' livestock. Lacombe, Large White, Landrace, Berkshire, Tamworth and other breeds are being introduced, and the number of pigs increased from 750,000 in 1960 to 950,000 in 1969.

In line with government encouragement of intensive production, battery hens are raised, and there are about 23 million fowls with 320 million eggs as the annual yield. The average poultry farm covers $1\frac{1}{2}$ acres. Farmers have been taught to vaccinate their own birds, and there is a pullorum disease eradication unit. The Chinese share the raising of poultry to some extent with the Malays, and run all the pig farms, with which for religious reasons Malays may not be associated. Mutton and beef are almost entirely imported, although Indian herdsmen raise cattle by the roadside in small numbers. A few families keep goats. There are one or two crocodile farms, for which the eggs are usually imported, and the skins are made up and sold in the Stamford Road area.

Orchids

In recent years orchids have become one of the most profitable export crops, and the 'Orchid Mile', extending alongside the canal between the Dunearn and Bukit Timah Roads, is devoted to the sale and cultivation of the flowers by private firms. The value of cut flowers exported is almost $1 million (£135,000; US $333,000) annually, and the main varieties, exported to Europe and Hong Kong, are Arachnis Maggie Oei, Aranda Galistan, Aranda Peter Ewart, Aranda Wendy Scott, Aranda Deborah, Aranda Nancy, Aranthera James Storie, Aranthera Mohamed Haniff, Oncidium Golden Shower and most varieties of Dendrobium.

FISHERIES

About 60,000 long tons of fish are consumed yearly in Singapore, but about 70 per cent of this is imported, nine-tenths of it from West Malaysia. Until recently, fishing was entirely carried on in traditional and uneconomic ways, and much of this persists. Thus, most of the 3–4,000 long tons caught by inshore fishermen annually is trapped by means of simple gear such as lift nets, beach seines, sunken seines, drift nets, fish pots and handlines, and the *kelongs* or palisade traps dotted around the coast (and forbidden to women for superstitious reasons). Of about 1,000 small inshore fishing vessels, only half are mechanised, and between them these account for 75 per cent of the local catch. There are about 2,000 licensed fishermen in Singapore, including inshore and offshore, but there are probably 1,000 more fishing unlicensed and part-time.

The DBS is involved in efforts to develop the offshore fishing industry, which supports about 250 large vessels of 40–100ft in length, with a tonnage of 30–100 gross tons. With the use of long lines, troll lines, and trawl nets, about 13,000 long tons of offshore fish are caught annually in the South China Sea and the Indian Ocean. Offshore fishermen are quite often attacked by pirates, and run the danger of imprisonment with confiscation of their vessels if they stray beyond territorial waters.

In February 1969 the Jurong fishing port was opened to make the focal point of the Singapore fishing industry. Local and foreign vessels land their catches at the 700ft wharf which, with its 16ft draught, can accommodate some of the largest fishing vessels. The Jurong port is a marketing and distributing centre handling about 140 long tons daily, and several processing plants have been set up there. It is also an *entrepôt* for salted and dried fish.

In 1969 the Marine Fisheries Research Department of the South East Asian Fisheries Development Centre, a regional project, was established at Changi, and is active in the search for new fishing grounds and the study of fisheries resources. The Fishing Training Centre, also at Changi, trains fishing technicians for offshore and deep-sea fishing. It has two training vessels, and holds deck courses to train navigators and fishermen and an engineering course to train fishing vessel engineers.

There are a number of freshwater fish farms which cultivate the common carp, the grass carp, the silver carp, the bighead carp, and the Javanese carp in ponds for local consumers, but the production is very small. Prawns are cultivated in a way virtually peculiar to Singapore : the post-larvae of the Paeneid prawns enter the mangrove swamps with the incoming tide, and are then trapped in shallow ponds. The prawns are caught in a falling tide in a conical net placed in a sluice channel. More important to Singapore's economy than either carp or prawns is the growth of the ornamental fish industry, an important source of foreign exchange with an export value of over $5 million (£675,675; US $1·7 million) yearly. The Freshwater Fisheries Laboratory at Sembawang carries out research on the breeding of ornamental aquarium fish.

10   SOCIAL SERVICES

AT the time of independence the Singapore government was faced with a great number of problems in the areas of health, social welfare and education. Its response shows a recognition of two factors in particular : the interconnection of these areas and the need to achieve the maximum results in the shortest possible time. In health, education and social welfare alike, the government is hampered by a shortage of trained staff. Projects for social improvement not only jostle with each other for funds, but have had to take second place to Singapore's economic development, without which they could not continue to run. Such difficulties, common to all developing societies, have been further complicated by the multi-racial composition of the people. Language, for example, is an obviously sensitive area in education; medicine is another, owing to the differences between Chinese and western practice, and to Malay reliance on the the *bomoh*, the traditional medicine man.

In the face of these problems the government has used an extremely practical approach which lays emphasis on the ideal of 'the rugged society' and the importance of educating the rising generation in ways of self-help. Educational programmes encourage mutual tolerance and the cultivation of full bilingualism.

In the rush to pull the nation into the twentieth century, something is necessarily lost. Education, for example, is still examination-ridden, partly because of the Chinese tradition, but partly because professional qualifications are tangible proofs of success, unlike the personal qualities fostered by a broader and more leisurely style of education. Although education is not compulsory, parents scramble to get places for their children in private kindergartens, which often attempt to teach reading and writing to children barely three years old. As in most western countries, a hard core of the deprived remains. In Singapore these are urban squatter families unable to afford the rent of HDB flats, and those old and infirm people whose relatives have not observed the Asian tradition that the family is the first and most reliable source of social welfare. The magnificent housing programme which in other ways gives so much to the people is accelerating the break-up of the old family units. Their replacement by a deeper concern for the individual is still in its infancy : in recent years there has been some anxiety over the lack of voluntary workers for charitable organisations. Yet the new killer diseases at the top of the list in Singapore are those of an affluent society, namely, heart disease and cancer, and the average citizen is better housed, better fed and better educated then ever before. The mainspring of social development remains, in Singapore, the education of society at large, and, with roughly 40 per cent of the population under the age of fifteen, this is a vast, expensive undertaking.

EDUCATION

Educational institutions in Singapore, before independence, grew up piecemeal. Raffles had an ambitious scheme to set up an institution for the education of 'the sons of the higher order of natives and others', and to teach the native languages to anyone who wished it. With this in mind a building was erected in 1823 at the corner of Bras Basah Road and Beach Road, but the building proved unsound and the scheme unsuccessful. However, the school, known as Raffles Institution, and one of the most famous in the Far East, was later rebuilt on the same spot and used continuously until it was pulled down and the establishment removed to Irwell Bank Road in 1971. Its management was first taken over by the government in 1903.

The first successful schools in Singapore were the mission schools, the earliest one of which was set up in 1822 by the London Missionary Society. By 1834 two American missionaries, Reverend Parker and Reverend Tracy, were running a Chinese Free School for Boys in the centre of the town, and in 1843 the Church of England Zenana Girls' Mission School was established, later to become the Anglo-Chinese School. The first Tamil school was started in 1859 at Waterloo Street as St Francis Xavier Malabar School, and the Portuguese mission set up a school for boys and a convent for girls in 1885. The mission schools taught for the most part in English.

The colonial government established schools in the English and Malay media, but Chinese and Tamil were left to private initiative. Of the four language streams, only Chinese and English had developed full secondary education before World War II, and in the postwar period there was tertiary education only in English until the founding of Nanyang University in the 1950s.

Before 1932 children could be sold in Singapore as household slaves, and Janet Lim describes in her book *Sold for Silver* how this happened to her when she was brought from China at the age of eight. Eventually she was looked after at a mission school. Today, as a result of a vast building programme, there are school places for all those who want them, and one of the most pleasant sights in Singapore is the swarm of black-haired, dark-eyed children with skins of every shade of brown, black and yellow, hurrying along to school in carefully pressed uniforms, with shirts and blouses of dazzling whiteness. Primary school education is free between the ages of six and fourteen for the children of Singapore citizens. Between 1 January 1969 and 31 March 1970, $198,712,470 (£26,853,000; US $66,237,490) was set aside for annually recurring educational expenses, and $30,850,000 (£4,182,432; US $10,283,300) for development expenditure, most of it on technical education. Almost all of this was government money; very little comes in the form of foreign aid.

SINGAPORE

In 1970 over a quarter of the total population, amounting to 514,080 children, attended school full-time. More than 4,800 of them attended registered kindergartens; 363,518 attended primary schools, and 145,740 secondary schools. Primary and secondary schools together totalled 550, of which 266 were run by the state, 267 were government-aided, and 17 were private. Government-aided schools receive up to 50 per cent of their development costs and a per capita grant, varying with the number of students, towards total costs. The 18,798 Singapore teachers, of whom 98·3 per cent worked in government and government-aided schools, represented almost 1 per cent of the total population. Nevertheless, the shortage of teachers and the crash building programme have made a double session necessary for primary and secondary schools : different sets of children are taught in the same buildings and by the same staffs in the mornings and the afternoons respectively, though in 1971 a tentative move back to the single-session system began in some technical schools.

Language is a key issue in Singapore educational programmes. Before World War II, the division between the various races of the community was emphasised by the existence of schools separately using the four main languages for instruction, and almost exclusively attended by children sharing the same native language. In 1947 the colonial government adopted a Ten Years' Programme on which to base educational development, and with it the principles of equal opportunity for all races, full primary education, and the encouragement through education of public spirit and the capacity for self-government. The choice of language was left to the parents, but in practice the government encouraged the expansion of education in English, seeing it as a politically neutral language with which the various races might be welded together in preparation for independence. Parity of treatment for the four languages was first accepted in a White Paper of 1956, published as a result of an all-party committee. Nevertheless, in 1952 the Chinese school enrolment (74,104)

182

exceeded that of all the other language streams combined (Malay 8,579; English 63,386; Tamil 1,205; total 73,170).

Today, parents may choose the language of instruction for their child, but all pupils must learn at least one second language, and this is always English where the first language is not. Many parents train their children in bilingualism early, by sending them to a kindergarten which employs a different language from that used at home. Schools using each of the four main languages as the medium of instruction exist at both primary and secondary level, but since 1960 the trend has been to build bilateral schools, with all four language streams under the same roof. Whatever the medium of instruction, the curriculum and the contents of the syllabus are held in common, and the Singapore-Cambridge School Certificate examination, taken in the fourth year of secondary education, is the same in all four languages.

Language	1959		1967		1970	
	Number	*Per Cent*	*Number*	*Per Cent*	*Number*	*Per Cent*
English	163,486	50·9	304,651	58·9	317,335	62·3
Chinese	140,231	43·6	175,278	33·8	162,111	31·8
Malay	15,804	5·0	36,142	7·0	28,340	5·6
Tamil	1,456	0·5	1,814	0·3	1,472	0·3
Total	320,977	100·0	517,885	100·0	509,258	100·0

SCHOOL ENROLMENT IN SINGAPORE

One of Singapore's great educational problems is that parity of treatment among the languages is easier to accept than to put into practice : many principals and assistant teachers are not themselves effectively bilingual, and techniques of teaching a second language are often poor. The real difficulty is, as so often for Singapore, the desire to encompass several different aims simultaneously : in this case, universal basic education, multilingualism, and the high level of technical education necessary to sustain Singapore's economic growth. The position is complicated further by the fact that English, the language of industrial modernisation, is *primus inter pares*. In the past few years, the economic importance of English has apparently been recognised by the decrease in the percentage of enrolment in Chinese, Malay and Tamil schools, though at the same time there has been a rise in the number of those studying Chinese as a second language, who in 1970 numbered about 200,000. The proportion of those learning Tamil, even as a second language, is so small as to present administrative problems.

At six years of age, the child begins six years of instruction at the primary school, after which he sits for a leaving examination. If successful, he proceeds to a secondary school. If he is unsuccessful, he may try again until he is over fourteen, when his formal education is finished unless he applies for the two-year course run by the Adult Education Board, or goes on to vocational training.

At secondary level, academic or technical or commercial subjects may predominate, or, if the school is bilateral, it will have both technical and academic streams. From 1969, it was made compulsory for all boys and 50 per cent of the girls in the first two years of secondary education to return to school outside the normal hours to take two workshop subjects for three hours weekly. This is part of the government drive to raise the number and expertise of Singapore's future technicians.

The full secondary course lasts for four years in all. Students wishing to take the Higher School Certificate proceed to preuniversity courses of one or two years, which are available in all languages but Tamil at most secondary schools and at the National Junior College, set up in 1969. The college, established to provide an unusually small student-teacher ratio, and to supplement morning lectures with afternoon tutorials and practical work, had, in April 1970, 971 students, two-thirds of them taking science and the rest the arts course. Some 600 of these students were in the Chinese stream.

The system is highly competitive, and in some ways the schools, with their emphasis on examination-passing, on sports and cadet corps, and on enthusiasm for extra-curricular activities, recall the

English ideal of the thirties. There, however, the comparison stops, for Singapore is concerned with producing a meritocracy, not an élite class. Yet the Singapore educational system, though geared by means of scholarships and grants to help any naturally academic child, however poor, has as yet no place for the 'odd-ball'; because of the hit-and-miss nature of their practical value to society, the non-conformist and the open-ended thinker are luxuries this developing society has not so far been able to afford. Pupils often complain of mental indigestion, and of having so much cramming to do that they never have time to think. There are signs that the Ministry of Education is aware of this, and a curriculum advisory committee has been set up with a director of research, to introduce experimental projects in selected schools. Some choice of subjects has from 1970 been given in addition to the compulsory subjects in secondary schools.

In the Asian tradition, teachers enjoy the esteem of society, but in recent years have shown a good deal of dissatisfaction. They complain of low salaries, a heavy burden of extra-curricular and holiday duties, and the timidity of many school principals in the face of the inspectorate. Puritanism is part of the general scene in Singapore, but the narrowness and lack of independence found in some staffrooms is a legacy both of colonial times and of the Chinese tradition. The republic must have one of the few schools in the world where the staff, not merely the pupils, were persuaded by the principal to begin wearing uniform.

There is only one training college for teachers. It is multi-lingual and trains about 2,000 students yearly, six-sevenths of them non-graduates. There has never yet been a sufficient supply of well-trained teachers : Singapore's need for them has to compete with the necessity to call young men up for national service, and with the higher salaries and shortage of educated personnel in industry. At the lower levels of secondary education, untrained teachers with Higher School Certificate are permitted to teach general subjects. An educational television service was introduced in 1967 in order to overcome the shortage of specialists. It is in the charge of the Ministry of Education, although its programmes are telecast by the radio television service of the Ministry of Culture. Every secondary school has a television set.

Technical education

The 1960s were devoted to expansion of the educational system in general, but in the 1970s the emphasis is on the technical side, as part of the government's plan to industrialise. In addition to the General Education Department of the Ministry of Education, which supervises all academic schools at primary and secondary level, and the teaching of general subjects, there is a parallel Department for Technical Education. This supervises bilateral and technical schools, vocational institutes and industrial training centres, and the Singapore Technical Institute. Three hundred and sixty-six new posts were created for this department in 1969, and $16·8 million (£2·05 million; US $5·6 million) set aside for development expenditure in technical education. A National Industrial Training Council has been set up to promote liaison between education and industry, with the Minister for Education as its chairman and the Ministers of Finance and Labour as members. The council is served by the director of technical education and two deputy directors, one for technical education and the other for industrial training.

There are three vocational institutes and four industrial training centres, which have over 4,000 students between them, and which give training to young men and women for semi-skilled work in industry. Courses range from building construction to electronics assembly and work in the metal trades. The bridge between these industrial training institutions and the technical colleges is the Singapore Technical Institute, set up in 1969. At present it has about 300 students, but when fully established will take 1,000 full-time and 1,000 part-time students. It has a school of nautical studies and a school of industrial technology.

A good deal of re-organisation took place in the 1960s, in the course of which independent institutions were taken over fully or partly by the government, sometimes mainly because their students had been involved in political agitation. One such is the Ngee Ann Technical College. This was established in 1963 as a private enterprise set up by a Teochew clan association, the Ngee Ann *Kongsi*. It began as a college teaching technical, domestic science and language courses to Chinese secondary school leavers, but in 1967 it was re-organised as a community college and later offered degree courses. Now administered by a council including representatives of the *kongsi* and the government, it was named a technical college in 1968. At present it gives diploma courses only, and has departments of mechanical engineering and industrial electronics and a department of commerce. It has some 600 students, about 100 of them from Malaysia and other surrounding countries.

The chief burden of higher technical education under the recent re-organisation has been laid on the Singapore Polytechnic. This, established in 1954, now offers full-time courses at technician diploma and certificate levels, in civil, electrical, mechanical, electronics and production engineering, rubber and plastics technology, building draughtsmanship, quantity surveying, marine engineering phase one, and pre-sea marine radio officers' and industrial technicians' courses. It also offers day release and evening classes, and of a total of about 4,000 students in 1970 754 studied full-time.

The Universities

There are two universities, reflecting that division of the Chinese community into Chinese-educated and English-educated, a force in Singapore politics, which was begun under the colonial government and its mission schools, and perpetuated to some extent by the existence of two Chinese communities, the Straits-born and the China-born.

'Suitability certificates' are still required from the principal of their secondary school for all students at a higher level, and act as a guarantee of political reliability. The retention of the law covering these certificates is a sore point with many citizens, but in so small a place, political non-conformists are relatively easy to keep track of, and government control over all scholarships, including those offered by outside bodies, discourages student rebellion.

The University of Singapore had its origin in 1905, when King Edward VII College of Medicine was set up. The college was amalgamated in 1949 with Raffles College (set up in 1929 for the study of arts and sciences) to form the University of Malaya. In 1959 the University of Malaya was divided into two largely autonomous sections, one of them in Kuala Lumpur, and in 1962 the Singapore establishment became completely separate, forming the University of Singapore.

Total enrolment in 1970 was 4,433 students, of whom 1,456 were women. Degree courses include arts, accountancy, architecture, building, estate management, business administration, science, social sciences, law, engineering, medicine, dentistry and pharmacy, and there are diploma courses in business administration, education, public health, fisheries, and social studies. Higher degrees are awarded in most faculties and schools.

There are a number of research centres attached to the University of Singapore, including a Cancer Research Centre, Economic Research Centre, UK Science Research Council, Radio Research Substation (in association with the University's Department of Physics), UNESCO Regional Marine Biological Centre and WHO Immunology Research and Training Centre.

The Nanyang University, built in distinctively Chinese style, with dipping green roof tiles and ornamental balustrades, was established in 1953 as a private institution for higher education in the medium of Chinese, but did not begin functioning until 1956. The Nanyang University Ordinance came into effect in 1959 as a first step to drawing the university into Singapore's recognised educational system. In 1964 it was agreed between the government and the university council that the Nanyang should be supported financially by the government on the same basis as the University of Singapore, and that it should be re-organised in order to take students in all language streams. The Nanyang University has been considered at various times a centre of disaffection. Moreover, to have an exclusively Chinese university in a country too small to support similar institutions in all four languages was thought to promote an unfortunate polarisation of the English-educated and Chinese-educated cultural groups. Nanyang seems more likely to produce genuinely bilingual students than the University of Singapore, since English is virtually essential in public life, whilst the necessity to learn Chinese is less obvious. It is possible therefore that Singapore's future leaders will come from the ranks of the Nanyang rather than from the University of Singapore. The prime minister has pointed out that there are special opportunities in industrial management for Nanyang graduates since they will be able to speak the languages of labour and of foreign experts alike if they emerge truly bilingual.

Nanyang University comprises colleges of arts, science and commerce, plus a College of Graduate Studies which consists of the institute of Asian studies, mathematics, natural sciences and business studies. In 1970 its total enrolment was 2,209. It supports a language centre giving courses in Mandarin, English, Malay, Japanese, French and German and using modern language laboratory techniques. In 1969 a computer centre was set up.

Singapore is a member of the South East Asian Ministers of Education Organisation (SEAMEO), among the projects of which is a regional English language centre situated in Singapore. It provides courses in the teaching of English as a foreign language for key educational personnel from SEAMEO member countries, which include Indonesia, Laos, Malaysia, the Philippines, Singapore, Thailand and Vietnam.

SOCIAL WELFARE

The first relief measure ever undertaken by a Singapore government was an emergency relief scheme brought in to cope with post-World War II conditions, with a maximum allowance of $20 (£2·70; US $7) per month per family. This later became the foundation of public assistance, introduced on a permanent basis in 1951. The genesis of many social welfare arrangements took place in the late 1940s and early 1950s, under the colonial government. In 1949, Singapore became the first country in the Far East to grant allowances to TB sufferers. In 1949, legislation was enacted to set up juvenile and probation court services, and to expand welfare services for children and young people. In 1954, a youth welfare service was introduced, to guide and advise youth organisations on their development. In 1953 the first large community centre was built at Upper Serangoon, and in 1960 the People's Association took over the function of promoting youth welfare and community development.

The People's Association now administers 186 community centres, a number of holiday camps and 380 fee-paying kindergartens. Its centres are run by management committees drawn from a cross-section of local residents, more often the non-English speaking elements of the community. The centres are seen everywhere in Singapore, their basketball pitches floodlit by night, and a crowd gathered round the television set.

Social welfare has a relatively low priority in the Singapore budget. It receives about $10 million (£1·35 million; US $3·3 million) for its annual expenditure, excluding any capital projects, and is administered by the Social Welfare Department of the Ministry of Social Affairs. The amount of money and the number of families helped by public assistance has steadily declined since 1964. There is no doubt that the government counts every penny, preferring to put it into economic development, but the decline is due much more to the general rise in the standard of living and the fall in unemployment. In 1960 the amount spent on public assistance was $7,398,179 (£999,750; US $2,466,060); in 1969 it was $4,676,720 (£631,989; US $1,558,907). In 1960 the monthly average of families assisted was 22,387; by 1969 it had fallen to 13,965. People eligible for allowances are Singapore

Page 191 Industry and horticulture: *(above)* metal products factory, Jurong; such relatively unsophisticated establishments, common in the sixties, are now giving way to industries requiring high technological skills, including electronics and precision engineering; *(below)* Chinese market gardeners tending their crops: they wear wide-brimmed hats against the tropical sun

Page 192 *(above)* The High Court Building, fronting the Padang; *(below)* sailing and steamships in the Tanjong Pagar Co's dry docks, 1894

citizens who are aged, chronically sick, physically and mentally handicapped, widows and orphans, and unemployed persons over fifty-five, or certified unfit for work, or having unemployed dependants. The maximum allowance is $60 (£8·15; US $20) a month per household.

Under the TB treatment allowance scheme, a monthly maximum of $120 (£16·30; US $40) per household is payable for up to twenty-four months to sufferers from TB whose recovery is progressing. In 1960 the total amount paid out to 2,186 families was $2,049,688 (£276,984; US $683,229); in 1969, 413 families were helped with $360,037 (£48,653; US $120,012).

The Social Welfare Department is also responsible for ad hoc relief measures. These are normally necessary only when there are floods or large fires. The risk of either is now being reduced, that of floods by extensive PWD schemes and that of fire by urban renewal and rehousing.

The Social Welfare Department is responsible for twelve residential institutions, nine children's centres and ten crèches. The children's centres provide some informal education and vocational training for children from eight to fifteen years who are school dropouts from poor families. The crèches look after the children of working parents during the day, and in all can take 900 children up to the age of six. One dollar (14p; US 33c) a morning is charged for the service, and 50 cents for the afternoon. The Social Welfare Department also deals with the care and protection of children and young persons, including their reception into places of safety, the investigation and prosecution of cruelty, and sometimes casework to assist the legal authorities with applications for adoption. There is a boarding-out scheme for children, including the mentally deficient, up to ten years old.

Since 1965, destitute persons may not be imprisoned for destitution alone, but they may be required by the authorities to reside in a welfare home or may apply to do so. The standard of such homes remains minimal.

A very great deal of the social welfare work of the republic rests as the responsibility of voluntary organisations. The work is co-ordinated by the Singapore Council of Social Service, which receives about $10,000 (£1,350; US $3,330) annually from the government to meet its administrative expenses. Set up after the end of World War II as an advisory body to the government, it was re-organised in 1958 with membership drawn from all voluntary welfare bodies in Singapore. It has ninety-one full-member organisations. It is these organisations which, with some government assistance, are largely responsible for looking after the republic's crippled, spastic and retarded children, the blind, the deaf, the paralysed and the incurably ill. In these voluntary organisations, which depend mainly on public support, there is a very high ratio of untrained workers, and the same is true of the Social Welfare Department itself.

There are no contributory schemes of social insurance applicable to the population at large, though private schemes abound and the organisations operating them must be registered with the government. In 1955, however, the Central Provident Fund (CPF) was established by the government. This, essentially a savings fund to make provision for the old age of the current working population, levies compulsory contributions from both employers and employees. The contribution for workers earning below $200 (£27·25; US $67) monthly is 10 per cent of wages; for those earning above $200 it ranges between 13 and 16 per cent of wages, the maximum joint contribution being $300 (£40·80; US $100) a month. Government servants with pensionable status are outside the scheme, but it applies to the self-employed. From 1968 workers have been able to use their CPF savings to buy government-built flats, and the money may be drawn out by the employee at age fifty-five, or if he suffers mental and physical incapacity, or by the next of kin after his death. The CPF is administered by the Ministry of Labour. In October 1970 there were 626,500 accounts with balances in the fund amounting to $711,873,606 (£96,199,130; US $237,291,202) and 34,098 employers were registered by the Board.

HEALTH

In Singapore there are many tiny clinics whose windows display traditional Chinese medicines, and the ancient Chinese practice of acupuncture is widely known. Recently the *sinsehs* (practitioners of Chinese medicine) have been pressing for legal recognition of their status. The Malays of the *kampong* consult the *bomoh*, who is something between a medicine man and a priest, and who works by means of herbs, divination and exorcism. More affluent Malays also consult him in cases where they are not entirely satisfied with treatment by their general practitioner. In spite of this, it has rightly been said that 'the whole history of the health services in Singapore is that of the acceptance of western medicine'.

Tuberculosis	458
Malignant neoplasms	1,596
Cerebrovascular disease	1,041
Heart diseases	1,430
Pneumonia	847
Hypertensive disease	357
Motor vehicle accidents	280

PRINCIPAL CAUSES OF DEATH 1970

Today the average life expectancy is 64·4 years, compared with 36 in some other parts of Asia, and the crude death rate (1970) is 5·2 per 1,000 of population. Buckley, Cameron, and other nineteenth-century writers speak of Singapore as a relatively healthy place for Europeans, despite periodic outbreaks of smallpox and cholera, for which each section of the community had its trusted remedy: thus in 1851 an official publication advised that the body be briskly 'champooed', after which a glass of brandy and pepper, followed by a drink of pounded ginger and salt in hot water was to be taken. The rickshaw pullers, on the other hand, put their faith in demon-scaring ceremonies, which they carried out continuously for as much as ten days, as in

1907. The only dissident voice about the healthiness of Singapore was that of Rudyard Kipling, who remarked that 'people in Singapore are deadwhite—as white as Naaman—and the veins on the back of their hands are painted in indigo', and who went on to say that 'typhoid fever appears to be one gate of death, as it is in India; also liver'.

Hospitals

The first western-trained doctor, Thomas Prendergast, was brought out to serve the East India Company, and coped as best he might with the ulcers, sores, cholera, fever and dysentery with which the jungle-clearing labourers of Raffles' new settlement were afflicted. Lunatics were put into the jail with the convicts until 1840, when they were separately housed. Whilst the affluent of all nationalities were looked after in their own homes, a small hospital for seamen and an insanitary *attap* bungalow used as a pauper hospital were the only provision made for the rest of the community before 1844. In that year, when the *Singapore Free Press* was reporting that 'a number of diseased Chinese, lepers and others, frequent almost every street in town', Tan Tock Seng, a wealthy Chinese, gave money for the erection of a hospital for the poor. It was built at the foot of Pearl's Hill, but at first no water was provided and the morning after it opened the inmates were found 'washing their sores in the puddles outside'. The site was never satisfactory, and later the hospital was moved near Balestier Road. Rebuilt in 1909, it is now a government general hospital beginning to specialise in TB and chest cases.

The Seamen's Hospital, the site of which was constantly moved, was next to the present Outram Road General Hospital when Joseph Conrad was a patient there in 1887, having been injured by a falling spar, an incident he transfers to the life of Lord Jim.

The establishment of Singapore's first College of Medicine in 1905, the cost of building which subscribed largely by Chinese members of the public, gave an impetus to the development of medical facilities. After World War I a big hospital building programme was effected, the municipal isolation hospital, the Middleton, having been put up in 1913. Outram Road General Hospital and the Trafalgar Home, the leprosy hospital, were both completed in 1926. The present mental hospital, renamed Woodbridge in 1951, followed in 1927, and Kandang Kerbau Maternity Hospital, which remained the only government centre for gynaecology until a unit was established at Thomson Road in 1969, was built in 1928.

The aftermath of war led a second time to an acceleration in the provision of facilities, and a government ten-year medical plan between 1949 and 1959 helped modernisation and expansion. Thomson Road Hospital was built in 1959.

Today, there are seventeen government hospitals, four of them being police, prison or remand home hospitals, and two of them (Alexandra and Sembawang) having been acquired in 1971 as a result of the British armed forces' withdrawal. Before the acquisition of these extra hospitals, the balance was that government hospitals provided 6,959 beds, and the six private hospitals provided 861, the total being 7,820, a ratio of 3·9 per 1,000 of population. The six private hospitals included the two British forces' hospitals now taken over, one 120-bed hospital for the RAF at Changi, and three others entirely within the private sector.

Disease

The pattern of disease has changed in Singapore over the years, notably since the end of World War II, and the respective functions of the hospitals have changed with it. Before 1945 there was little in the way of preventive medicine, and between 1907 and 1910 there was an average of 2,000 deaths yearly from malaria alone. In 1906 the introduction of a sewer system was decided on and the modern framework had been laid down by 1930, a concerted effort having also been made at anti-malarial drainage. In 1919 it was stated in the history of Singapore written to mark its centenary that the main causes of death 'for many years' had been 'phthisis, malaria, dysentery and beri-beri'. By

197

the 1950s the incidence of infectious diseases, of leprosy, enteric infections and TB was waning, but the general hospital wards were acutely overcrowded. There is now only one hospital for infectious diseases in Singapore—the Middleton, with 250 beds—but Thomas Road Hospital, originally built for the chronic sick, has been made into an additional general hospital. The most pressingly overcrowded, as in many western countries, is the mental hospital, which has an official complement of 2,029 beds, but an average daily occupancy 30 per cent in excess of this. The Middle Road Hospital treats VD and skin diseases, a rather curious combination which dates from colonial times. St Andrew's Orthopaedic Hospital has 120 beds for the care and treatment of children with post-polio deformities. Work with lepers, the mentally ill or defective, and the crippled continues to be hampered by traditional attitudes of rejection, though officially such ideas are discouraged. Some men and women cured of leprosy, for example, stay on at the Trafalgar Home because they are not accepted in the communities from which they originally came. On the other hand, the number of physically handicapped in employment is rising steadily as a result of a government campaign.

Of the dangerous internationally quarantinable diseases, only smallpox, in 1959, and El Tor cholera (four times in eight years) have made their appearance in the postwar years. Common tropical diseases such as malaria, filariasis and ankylostomiasis are under control, and there has been no poliomyelitis in recent years. Nearly 95 per cent of the population are served by piped water, which it is safe to drink from the tap. The Public Health Division of the Ministry of Health includes an epidemiology unit, which makes regular checks on rats in the port area to keep Singapore clear of bubonic plague.

The number of TB patients fell from 358 per 100,000 of population in 1959 to 186 in 1969, and the mortality rate in TB from 39·7 to 20·8 per 100,000. This improvement is partly a result of the child health programme, according to which BCG vaccination has been given to over 90 per cent of all newborn babies in the republic.

Disease	Cases Notified*			Cases per 100,000 Inhabitants
	City	*Rural*	*Total*	
Chicken-pox	721	680	1,401	69·45
Puerperal Fever	238	195	433	21·47
Typhoid Fever	97	128	225	11·16
Leprosy	120	74	194	9·62
Malaria	142	160	302	14·97

* Tuberculosis and venereal diseases are not notified to the Public Health Division

MAJOR DISEASES NOTIFIED TO THE PUBLIC HEALTH DIVISION IN 1969

Clinics

After independence in 1959, the government opened a network of twenty-seven outpatient dispensaries and five staff dispensaries scattered throughout the island. These, which give a normal general practitioner's service, and cover minor injuries and surgical procedures, were intended to relieve the pressure on the hospitals, but in fact increased it by detecting new cases. At first, attendances, which now number over a million and a half annually, were free, but in 1964 a fee of 50 cents was levied for each attendance, and this has now been raised to $1·50 (21p; US 50 cents).

Infant mortality, which reached 345 per 1,000 in 1910, began to diminish when home visiting by nurses began in 1912; the first infant welfare clinics were opened in 1923. Today the infant mortality rate is 20·5 per 1,000 live births (1970). The Maternal and Child Health Service operates in fifty-two centres, at which prenatal and postnatal care are given, including a comprehensive vaccination and immunisation programme against TB, smallpox, diphtheria, whooping cough, tetanus and polio. About 60 per cent of expectant mothers attend annually, and in 1969, out of a total of 44,280 live births, 43,063 children were registered at the centres.

199

SINGAPORE

A Family Planning Association was formed in 1949 as a voluntary organisation, later subsidised by a government grant. Family planning is now under the guidance of the Singapore Family Planning and Population Board, a national agency, established in 1966 : 41 of its 49 clinics are housed in the same premises as the maternal and child health centres. In the same year it implemented a five-year plan with the object of lowering the birth rate from 32 per 1,000 inhabitants (1964) to below 20 in 1970. By 1969 the crude birth rate had dropped to 22·1 per 1,000, and it seems that the campaign has, temporarily at least, reached saturation point. However, it would appear that family planning has made considerable progress in all ethnic, cultural and religious groups, and if Singapore follows the pattern of other rapidly industrialising countries, the birth rate will continue to fall.

Public Health

Problems of health for Singapore are now largely identifiable with those of western countries, though the shortage of funds and trained personnel make its task more difficult. A committee on medical specialisation has been set up to advise on the order of priorities of development, and has already recommended the expansion of specialised facilities for neurosurgery, cardiothoracic surgery, plastic and reconstructive surgery, and nephrology. A number of such specialised units already exist, mainly at Outram Road Hospital, and in 1969 a radiotherapy department was completed, with two cobalt units. Singapore has an artificial kidney unit, an eye bank and a blood bank, and a public campaign has succeeded to some extent in overcoming the traditional and superstitious objections of the Chinese to donating blood.

Much depends on how far Singapore can absorb rising costs in the field of medicine. Sophisticated hospital equipment is extremely expensive. Services that were once provided at a nominal fee, at clinics and in the third-class wards of hospitals, now carry increased charges, which have been extended to midwifery and

200

dental services. The only major service which is still free is that of the maternal and child health centres.

In the belief that prevention is cheaper than cure, Singapore has pursued since 1968 a campaign to make it the cleanest city in the region. In that year the Environmental Health Act was introduced, to cover the entire range of government responsibilities and functions in public health, from public cleansing to the control and regulation of hawkers, markets, swimming pools, food establishments, offensive trades, crematoria, and public lavatories. All the necessary provisions were systematised and severe penalties provided, and the result, in the urban areas at least, is strikingly in evidence. Refuse is collected daily, and there are frequent public campaigns against mosquitoes and all forms of pollution. Food hawkers, until recently a picturesque sight as they wandered about with their portable foodstalls and ovens, driven by tricycles or slung from their shoulders, are gradually being moved to permanent sites with water and sanitation. Cigarette advertisements are banned, and the government is pursuing an active anti-smoking campaign, mainly through the medium of television. A Clean Air Act has recently been passed to deal with all forms of air pollution in trade and industry.

Dental Care

Fluoridation of water was begun in 1958 and is fully maintained, and there has been a significant drop in the incidence of dental decay as shown by schoolchildren over the past few years. In 1969 compulsory tooth-brushing was instituted in all primary schools, and all pupils were provided with a toothbrush and plastic mug at a charge of a few cents. About one-third of the primary school population of 370,000 gets full treatment and regular attention at the fifty-eight school clinics, at the maternal and child health centres and at units in charitable homes, but, like the school medical service, the dental service is still badly understaffed.

11   THE FUTURE

VISITORS returning to Singapore after an absence of five
years or more are invariably astonished at the extent to
which the island has changed in the meantime. In the
seventies, the pace grows faster and faster, and economic transformation brings ecological and social change in its wake. For
Singapore, planning, essential in all rapidly expanding cities, is
vital : its small size lays it open especially to the disastrous results
of careless thinking or failure to anticipate.

A master plan was in fact adopted by the government in 1958.
In 1961, after independence, United Nations technical assistance
was sought. The upshot has been a UN-assisted State and City
Planning Project which embraces a long-range plan implemented
in five-year stages, and which includes an urban renewal programme. The assumption is that by the 1990s, Singapore's population may reach three million, and may become stabilised at
about four million in the twenty-first century. Under the master
plan the need for full employment is recognised and so, apart
from housing, priority is given to the development of the port and
of the industrial estates, of the international airport and the
central area. Responsibility for conforming to the major provisions set out in the master plan rests with the Ministry of Law
and National Development. The Planning Department and the
Chief Building Surveyor's Department within the ministry control
physical development projects in the public and the private sec-
tors respectively. They are assisted by a master plan committee
and a development control committee.

Since 1967, various surveys have been undertaken to provide

the statistical basis for planning on an island-wide scale. Pieces of this fascinating jigsaw include a comprehensive survey of land use; studies of the development possibilities of the offshore islands; a forecast of housing demand; an estimate of future industrial land needs; a forecast of the number of motor vehicles in use; and an examination of the probable demand for commercial space, calculated according to the basic economic indicators. Most of these calculations extend at least to the 1990s.

Under the master plan, the purposes for which many areas of land are allotted are being changed, so that residential areas are being cleared to make highways, agricultural land is being turned into housing estates, and some areas are being set aside for light industry, for shopping complexes or for business districts. All this necessitates the resettlement of thousands of people, and most are to be accommodated in high-rise housing estates in the new towns. A high percentage of prewar buildings will disappear in the process.

The changes in Singapore's outward appearance are most obvious in the main business area, where the waterfront familiar to Somerset Maugham and little altered since the days of Joseph Conrad is being transformed. Collyer Quay is rapidly becoming a place of skyscrapers, hotel and shopping complexes up to twenty-nine storeys high, and huge car parks. Behind the waterfront, the old department stores and older shophouses of Raffles Place and the rest of Singapore's original business area are being systematically torn down and replaced by modern buildings of a kind which might belong to any large western city. The People's Park Shopping Complex, with thirty storeys, and the Bank of Singapore's fifty-storey office building will soon rub shoulders with other giants. The top of Fort Canning, latterly again a 'forbidden hill' because of its occupation by the military, is to be released for use as a public park, but the view from the top may well become one of skyscrapers rather than sea. The rebuilding of Chinatown and its transformation from an area of overcrowded shophouses and the colourful, endlessly shifting accompaniments of the life of the Chinese poor has begun; the first HDB project there, a twenty-one-storey complex, will be completed in 1972.

Where Singapore's most famous boys' school, Raffles Institution, has been pulled down, the Raffles Centre, a $100 million (£13·7 million; US $33·3 million) complex, is to rise. The 'Golden Mile' of shops, hotels and nightclubs along the reclaimed land on Nicoll Highway will be joined by a 'Golden Shoe' of office skyscrapers and bank buildings bounded by Fullerton Square, Shenton Circus and Telok Ayer Street. Orchard Road, in Cameron's day 'lined by tall bamboo hedges with thick shrubbery behind, and broken only here and there by the white portals at the entrance of the private avenues leading from it, or occasionally by a native hut or fruit shop', is now thronged from morning till night with shoppers and tourists, and will become more so as the latest of its international hotels rises into the sky.

Urban life is gradually spreading out, east and west of the main city area, and will eventually ring the island, though continued centralisation of the main administrative and business district is a key aspect of the master plan. Queenstown and Toa Payoh, now almost completed, were the first of the HDB satellite towns, and under the master plan will be joined by Woodlands in the north, Bedok in the east, and Telok Blangah in the southwest, in all to provide an additional 100,000 flats. About a third of the population now lives in such HDB flats; in 1972 the proportion is expected to be 70 per cent. The result of these developments under the master plan will be a high density belt west and east of the town towards Jurong and Changi respectively, plus a ring of heavy urban development round the other three sides of the central catchment area. After 1982, the shift in emphasis will be to the north, and the new industrial nuclei of Sembawang and Seletar.

Woodlands will be the town nearest the Causeway and the Malaysian border, and as such will have extensive customs and immigration facilities, but it will also be a dormitory area for people working in and around Bukit Timah. It is likely to take up to twenty years to complete, and will be as big as Queenstown and Toa Payoh combined. Telok Blangah, to be built near the south coast, to the west of the city area, will cover over 900 acres in one of Singapore's most attractive settings : HDB flats there may be of the most expensive type. Bedok, to be constructed around Kampong Chai Chee in the Upper Changi Road area, is being built on the site of hills which have been cut away to provide earth for coastal reclamation. Already the area presents the curious contrasts so common in Singapore : one may drive from the old shophouses of Changi village to the naked new housing blocks of Chai Chee, which rise from bulldozed desolation; set across from them huddle the one-storey *attap* houses of the *kampong*. The British military withdrawal has made land available for development at several points on the island, notably at Pasir Panjang, which by 1980 will become a major public housing and industrial complex, linking the city with Jurong.

Under the third five-year plan of 1970–5 (part of the master plan), further reclamation is to extend the coastline along the length of Nicoll Highway and Tanjong Rhu from the mouth of the Singapore river as far as Bedok. The final stage of reclamation, running from Bedok to Tanah Merah Besar, will yield 1,360 new acres. The scheme in its entirety will transform the coastline along the 12 miles from Collyer Quay to Changi, in all yielding 2,650 new acres. Land is also being drained in the north to provide for the Sembawang industrial estate.

Part of the reclaimed area from Tanjong Rhu to Bedok will carry a six-lane expressway, a section of the Pan-Island Expressway already under construction, and scheduled for completion in 1975. The expressway is designed to link the satellite towns with the city, and will have flyover interchanges at the main access points, but it is only a temporary solution to Singapore's traffic problems. It is estimated that by 1992, 60 per cent of Singapore households will own cars, and that the number of vehicles will reach 700,000, and plans are being discussed for a Mass Rapid

Transit System to cope with the increase. It is not yet known what form this will take.

The advent of jumbo jets and the expected increase in tourism mean that Singapore's airport facilities must be greatly expanded. Noise is a constant problem for those living anywhere near Paya Lebar airport, and it is possible that Changi will be developed as Singapore's premier international airport, since take-off and landing would be largely over the sea.

With such a limited land area to dispose of, the planners find themselves dealing with a puzzle to which there is no final and perfect answer : all they can do is to spend the maximum possible time in thought and research before beginning to re-shuffle the counters to obtain the greatest possible advantage for Singapore and its people. Into the tight, complicated plan must go new provisions for recreation and the extension of public utilities.

The nasty days of bucket-sanitation and night-soil collection may not finally depart until 1980, by which time it is envisaged that the whole island will be sewered. Daily water consumption is expected to rise to 150 million gal by 1975, and the construction of a desalinisation plant is being considered. Meanwhile, new reservoirs are being built at Kranji, Pandan and Upper Pierce and at the Upper Changi Road. Hand in hand with the provision of greater storage capacity for water goes the campaign to prevent water pollution, which is part of a recent government drive against pollution in all its forms.

In building a 58 acre marineland aquarium at Bedok, and a zoo at Seletar, as in developing the island of Sentosa as a holiday resort with a racetrack and casino, the government is trying to kill two birds with one stone : it hopes to provide something to attract tourists, and to increase the amenities for its own people. The snag, as shown already at the Jurong Bird Park, is that prices of admission geared to the tourist trade and the cost of upkeep are too high for the mass of Singapore's population. Open to more general appreciation are the new sandy beaches taking shape under reclamation between Bedok and Tanjong Rhu.

The cost of living is going up as a result of urban renewal, full employment and the increase in the number of expatriates living in Singapore, especially Americans following the oil boom : rents of middle-class flats and houses have risen by as much as 300 per cent in the past year or two, and land values with them. As for the poorer classes, it is estimated that more than three-quarters of the shack and shanty *kampongs* of Singapore will eventually be cleared, and the change of surroundings, whilst it will solve many problems, as of hygiene and land use, will undoubtedly produce new ones among their occupants. Some Singaporeans have already been moved twice as a result of land development plans, and many still living in the *kampongs* profess themselves unwilling to move to HDB flats. They are afraid of having to pay rent and water rates instead of, simply, an annual land tax as many of them do at present, of not being able to leave their doors open without fear of strangers; of being marooned in a concrete tower, away from trees and the friendly earth; of being cut off by distance and the demands of social hygiene from the various ways in which they eke out their incomes—such as raising chickens, running open-air stalls, and growing vegetables.

Under the old system, their numbers included many whose contribution to the national economy was marginal, being confined to such activities as hawking. The chances for them in the future seem to lie between increasing poverty, discontent and dehumanisation in the giant blocks of the new housing estates; and a vastly more prosperous future helped by Singapore's improved educational facilities and the jobs offered by an industrial economy. Which way they go will depend very much on how far they can be persuaded to enter willingly into the age of industrialisation, and, in the words of Lee Kuan Yew, 'to jettison parts of the value systems and culture patterns of the past'. The outcome is intimately involved with the division between the English-educated and the Chinese-educated, already referred to, and which, with China now a rising power with a seat at the UN, is likely to respond more sharply to international political developments. It is here that choice of language—on the part of parents choosing for their children as well as on the part of the government—becomes of paramount importance. Lee Kuan Yew, in giving the Fitzwilliam commemorative lecture for 1971 at the University of Cambridge, pointed out that a knowledge of the English language is an exceptionally valuable asset for all the developing countries, but one which must somehow be reconciled with pride in indigenous cultures. For Singapore, the problems are doubled : any violent swing towards China, culturally or politically (in Singapore this often means the same thing), will antagonise the Malays of the surrounding regions; too intense an emphasis on English and Malay at the expense of Chinese will alienate large sections of the population. At the same time, room must somehow be given for political dissent without extending it to political instability; both local and international reaction to the Singapore government's curbing of the Press in 1971 indicate some of the difficulties here.

Any government of Singapore, it is clear, must continuously perform a delicate balancing act, and this is as true of economic as of political matters. The path lies between failure to industrialise rapidly enough, and inability to cope with the problems brought by growing prosperity : the limits of wage control, the envy of Singapore's poorer neighbours, the effect on the community of the large numbers of immigrant workers from surrounding regions, and of Americans and Europeans, each with manners and morals which differ from those set as a standard in Singapore. Lee Kuan Yew himself has said that the students and workers of the less developed countries become confused when they see the young people of the West rejecting 'the Protestant work ethics . . . diligence, thrift and enterprise'. What he presumably fears is that the youth of Singapore will seek the trappings of western prosperity—the long hair, unisex clothing and penchant for endless amusement, including, for many, the taking of drugs—and lose their will for hard work in the process. In some respects Lee Kuan Yew's position thus forms a curious parallel, in spite of the difference in scale and political affinities, to that of Mao Tse Tung; each fears the rising generation will throw away what has been fought and toiled for, and each seeks to preserve his people from the contamination of the West though each is anxious to acquire its technical skills.

Unlike China, however, Singapore is in a position of special vulnerability to outside events, which may decide her ultimate fate despite the hard work and determination of her people. Lee Kuan Yew showed himself well aware of this when, again in 1971, he declared that if the government of South Vietnam were to collapse after the American withdrawal, the results could mean serious trouble for Singapore. The republic has emerged successfully from the dangers of *konfrontasi*, of separation from Malaysia, and, economically at least, from the British withdrawal. The mood of the place is one of confidence tempered with caution, as the scale of urban renewal and ambitious plans for the expansion of technical education bear witness. Singapore's role as an *entrepôt* port is declining, as both Indonesia and Malaysia begin to import and export directly from and to countries such as China; but the development of the oil industry has given remarkable impetus to Singapore's growth as an industrial port; and the change to the metric system, which began in 1971, is a sign of her readiness to participate to the full in world trade. Not for nothing do ordinary Singaporeans, as well as their prime minister, express their admiration of Japan for the extraordinary way in which her economy is overtaking that of the countries of Western Europe.

If the pressure of outside events allow her to survive intact, there is little doubt that, whatever else happens, Singapore will stand, despite her diminutive size, as remarkable in two ways, each of prime importance in the modern world: first, as a genuinely multi-racial state, and second, as an example of exceptional success in making the transition from developing country to industrial power.

GLOSSARY

Abbreviations

A., Arabic
C., Cantonese
Ch., Chinese
der., derived
esp., especially
Hok., Hokkien
H., Hindi
langs., languages

lit., literally
M., Malay
Mand., Mandarin
orig., originally
P., Portuguese
S., Singapore
T., Tamil

amah, Anglo-Indian from P. Female servant.

ang pow, Hok. Lit. red packet, used to describe gifts of money made to children at Chinese New Year, which are offered in red envelopes.

attap, M. Roofing thatch, usually made from the fronds of the nipah palm.

baba, common to many langs. In H. it means 'father, elderly person', but the character used for it in Ch. means 'man from the hills' ie one who has lost his own culture. Commonly used to designate a man from the Sino-Malay community of the Malacca Straits.

baju, M. Coat.

baju kurong, M. Woman's costume of long skirt and kneelength loose tunic.

batik, M. Method of colouring cloth by dyeing it after waxing. The word is often applied to the cloth itself.

belukar, M. Low scrub.

bersanding, M. Ceremony, orig. derived from Hindu ritual, at which the Malay bridegroom comes to fetch his bride and the couple sit in state.

bomoh, M. Native doctor.

bukit, M. Hill.

chandu, H. A prepared form of opium.

cheongsam, C. Lit. long dress. Ch. woman's dress, now usually worn kneelength, with high collar and side-slits to the thigh.

chettiar, T. A caste of South Indians from the district of Madras, who work as bankers, traders and moneylenders.

chichak, M. Common house lizard (*hemidactylus frenatus*).

Cristão, P. The *patois* spoken by Eurasian descendants of the P.

dhoby, H. Washerman.

ganja, H. A prepared form of cannabis resin; marijuana.

godown, Anglicisation of M. *gedong*, der. T. a warehouse.

haji, M. der. A. One who has made the pilgrimage to Mecca.

ikan, M. Fish.

jaga, M. Watchman.

jinn, M. der. A. A demon, a spirit.

joget moden, M. Malay dance performed to western music.

kain, M. A length of cloth, worn by women as a skirt, or by men tied round the waist of the *baju*.

kampong, M. A village settlement, orig. rural, but in S. often found in urban surroundings.

kathi, M. A registrar of Muslim marriages and divorces.

kavadi, T. An arched structure made of steel, supported by spikes fixed in the flesh of the shoulders; an instrument of self-mortification used at the Indian festival of Thaipusam.

kebaya, M. Close-fitting jacket worn by M. women.

kelong, M. A fixed-net method of catching fish at night; a bright light is used to lure the fish.

Kling, der. M. *keling*. A native of Madras; a South Indian.

koleh, M. A small boat with a white sail.

konfrontasi, M. Armed confrontation.

kongsi, Hok., also C., Hakka, Teochew. Partnership or association of any kind, but primarily used of Ch. guilds and secret societies.

kramat, M. Shrine.

kung hey fatt choy, C. Lit. wish happiness prosperity; Ch. New Year greeting.

lalang, M. Tall coarse grass (*imperata cylindrica*).

Majulah Singapura, M. May S. flourish.

merdeka, M. Freedom or independence.

Nan-yang, Mand. South Seas (used in the sense of South East Asia).

nyonya, M. Orig. a title used in addressing Ch. women, esp. the elderly; a woman of the Straits Ch. community.

orang laut, M. Lit. people from the sea. Aboriginal boat dwellers.

padang, M. An expanse of grass or treeless waste land; used by

Europeans to refer to playing fields. The Padang in S. is the stretch of grass used for games and parades in front of the city hall.

padi, M. Rice.

parang, M. A Malay chopper.

Pesta Sukan, M. S.'s annual festival of sport.

prahu, M. Used rather indiscriminately of Malay boats and small ships.

pulau, M. Island.

ronggeng, M. A dance orig. der. from the royal courts of Malaya.

samfoo, C. A Ch. woman's costume of tunic and trousers.

sepak takraw, M. A game with a rattan ball in which the use of arms and hands is forbidden.

songkok, M. A black velvet hat with stiffened sides, worn by M. men.

sungei, M. River.

tae kwan do, The Korean art of self-defence.

tongkang, M. A shallow-draft seagoing barge or lighter.

wayang, M. Theatrical performance, which may be given by puppets or by live actors.

yam sing, C. Lit. drink finish off. Bottoms up !

Yang di-Pertuan Negara, M. Head of State.

APPENDIX I

FEAST DAYS

Abbreviation : v., variable

New Year's Day, 1 January
Chinese New Year, v.
Hari Raya Haji, v.
Good Friday, v.
Labour Day, 1 May
Vesak Day, v.
National Day, 9 August
Deepavali, v.
Hari Raya Puasa, v.
Christmas Day, 25 December

MAIN FESTIVALS

Chinese

The observance of festivals is based on the old Chinese lunar calendar, with a cycle of sixty years

Chinese New Year, begins between 2 January and 18 February
Chap Goh Meh, 15th night after New Year
Ching Ming , 15th day of 3rd moon (early April)
Dragon Boat Festival, 5th day of 5th moon (late June)
Feast of the Seven Sisters, 7th day of 7th moon (mid August)
Mid Autumn or Mooncake Festival, 15th day of 8th moon (late September)
Double Ninth Festival, 9th day of 9th moon (mid October)

APPENDIX I

Muslim

The Muslim calendar is a lunar calendar of twelve months, alternating 29 and 30 days, and generally 11 days shorter than the Gregorian (solar) calendar

Hari Raya Haji, 10th day of Zulhijah (late February)

Birthday of the Prophet Mohammed, 12th day of Rabi'i'l-awal (June)

Ramadan, month of the annual fast, begins late October or early November

Hari Raya Puasa, 1st day of Shawal (late November or early December)

Indian

Ponggol (Harvest Day), v., January

Thaipusam, v., early February

Deepavali or Festival of Lights, v., early October

Nava Rathiri or Dasera, v., August

Onam, v., September

APPENDIX II

OFFSHORE ISLANDS WITHIN THE TERRITORIAL WATERS

Southern Islands

Name of Island	Area in Acres	Area in Sq Metres
Pulau Brani	123	497,763·34
Sentosa (formerly Pulau Blakang Mati)	712	2,881,361·77
Pulau Selegu	2	8,093·72
Pulau Hantu	8½	34,398·28
Pulau Sekijang Pelepah . . .	65	263,045·67
Pulau Sekijang Bendera (St John's Island)	83	335,889·08
Pulau Kusu (Peak Island) . . .	3	12,140·57
Pulau Tekukor	9	36,421·71
Pulau Bukom Besar	265	1,072,416·95
Pulau Bukom Kechil	74	299,467·38
Pulau Ular	1	4,046·86
Pulau Busing	10¾	43,503·71
Pulau Hantu Besar	5	20,234·28
Pulau Hantu Kechil	1	4,046·86
Pulau Semakau	175	708,199·87
Pulau Sekeng	18	72,843·42
Pulau Jong	1½	6,070·28
Pulau Sebarok	24	97,124·55
Pulau Sudong	25	101,171·41
Pulau Pawai	170	687,965·59
Pulau Biola	1	4,046·86
Pulau Satumu	1	4,046·86
Pulau Salu	1½	6,070·28
Pulau Berkas	—	—

APPENDIX II

Name of Island	Area in Acres	Area in Sq Metres
Pulau Senang	202	817,465·00
Pulau Seraya	127	513,950·77
Pulau Seburus Dalam	13	52,609·13
Pulau Seburus Luar	17	68,796·56
Pulau Mesmut Laut	4	16,187·43
Pulau Mesmut Darat	12	48,562·28
Pulau Ayer Merlimau . . .	310	1,254,525·49
Pulau Pesek	121	489,669·63
Pulau Meskol	15	60,702·85
Pulau Buaya	5	20,234·28
Pulau Ayer Merbau	246	995,526·68
Pulau Ayer Chawan	404	1,634,929·99
Pulau Sakra	82	331,842·23
Pulau Bakau	25	101,171·41
Pulau Semulon	42	169,967·97
Pulau Damar Laut	39	157,827·40
Sisters' Islands (2) . . .	2 and 4	8,093·71

Northern and Other Islands

	Acres	Sq Metres
Pulau Tekong Kechil . . .	220	890,308·41
Pulau Tekong Besar	4,429	17,923,527·10
Pulau Pergam	6	24,281·14
Pulau Merawang	4	16,187·43
Pulau Seletar	67	271,139·37
Pulau Serangoon	28	113,311·98
Pulau Ketam	83	457,294·77
Pulau San Yong Kong . . .	5	20,234·28
Pulau Sajahat	3	12,140·57
Pulau Ubin	2,506	10,141,422·11

Reef Islands

Sajahat Kechil	Bajan	Batu Belalai
Sekudu	Malang Panpan	Malang Siajao
	Umin	

INITIALS

Initials denoting organisations etc., as used in the text, are as follows :

ADB : Asian Development Bank
ASEAN : Association of South East Asian Nations
CPF : Central Provident Fund
DBS : Development Bank of Singapore
ECAFE : Economic Commission for Asia and the Far East
EDB : Economic Development Board
HDB : Housing Development Board
JTC : Jurong Town Corporation
MINDEF : Ministry of Defence
MSA : Malaysia-Singapore Airlines
NTUC : National Trades Union Congress
PAP : People's Action Party
PDF : People's Defence Force
PSA : Port of Singapore Authority
PUB : Public Utilities Board
PWD : Public Works Department
RAF : Royal Air Force
SAF : Singapore Armed Forces
SAFTI : Singapore Armed Forces Training Institute
SATU : Singapore Association of Trade Unions
SEAMEO : South East Asian Ministers of Education Organisation
SSRNVR : Straits Settlements Royal Naval Volunteer Reserve
TPDC : Tanjong Pagar Dock Company
UMNO : United Malay National Organisation
UN : United Nations

BIBLIOGRAPHY

The following bibliography is intended to give some idea of the range of material available for a study of Singapore, and therefore includes references to articles in learned periodicals, to government reports, and to collections of press cuttings in the reference department of the library of the University of Singapore. No attempt has been made to indicate material available in Malay, Chinese or Tamil. Further information may be obtained from the *Bibliography of Malaya; being a classified list of books wholly or partly in English relating to the Federation of Malaya and Singapore*, edited by H. R. Cheeseman, published for the British Association of Malaya by Longmans, Green and Co in 1959, and from *Books about Singapore*, published by the National Library, Singapore.

As yet, no professional historian has devoted his attention to the complete span of the history of modern Singapore, but it must be remarked that the histories and descriptive volumes published by amateurs, from Cameron onwards, are a marvellous treasury of anecdote and vignette, and exude that affection for and pride in Singapore which it seems to have inspired even from the earliest and most uncomfortable days. There is also a body of fiction which uses Singapore and its surrounding territories as a setting, and I have added a brief list of titles in this field.

ALLEN, B. M. *Malayan Fruits.* D. Moore, Singapore, 1967

ALLEN, R. *Malaysia: prospect and retrospect; the impact and aftermath of colonial rule.* Oxford University Press, London, 1968

AMERICAN UNIVERSITY, Washington. Foreign Areas Studies Division. *Area handbook for Malaysia and Singapore.* Co-authors : Bela C. Maday and others. US Govt Print Off, Washington, 1965

ANDERSON, P. *Snake Wine.* Chatto & Windus, London, 1955

ARASARATNAM, S. *Indian festivals in Malaya.* Dept of Indian Studies, University of Malaya, Kuala Lumpur, 1966

ATTIWILL, K. *The Singapore story.* F. Muller, London, 1959

BIBLIOGRAPHY

BARBER, N. *Sinister Twilight; The fall and rise again of Singapore.* Collins, London, 1968

BASTIN, J. and BENDA, H. S. *A History of Modern South East Asia.* Federal Publications, Kuala Lumpur and Singapore, 1968

BIRD, I. L. *The Golden Chersonese and the Way Thither.* Putnam, New York, 1883

BLYTHE, W. L. 'Historical sketch of Chinese labour in Malaya', *Royal Asiatic Society. Malayan Branch. Journal,* 1967

BOGAARS, G. *The Tanjong Pagar Dock Company, 1864–1905* and *Old Straits and New Harbour, 1300–1870,* by C. A. Gibson-Hill. Govt Print Off, Singapore, 1956

BOYCE, P. *Malaysia and Singapore in International Diplomacy.* Sydney University Press, 1968

BRACKMAN, A. C. *Southeast Asia's second front; the power struggle in the Malay archipelago.* Moore, Singapore, 1966

BRADDELL, R. *The Lights of Singapore.* Methuen, London, 1934

BRADDON, R. *The Naked Island.* Laurie, London, 1952

BUCKLEY, C. B. *An Anecdotal History of Old Times in Singapore 1819–1867.* Printed by Fraser & Neave, Singapore, 1902. University of Malaya Press, Kuala Lumpur, 1965

BURDON, T. W. 'The Fishing Methods of Singapore', *Royal Asiatic Society. Malayan Branch. Journal,* 27 no 2, March 1954 : 5–76

BURLING, R. *Hill Farms and Padi Fields: life in Mainland SE Asia.* Prentice-Hall, Englewood Cliffs, NJ, 1965

CADDY, F. *To Siam and Malaya, in the Duke of Sutherland's Yacht 'Sans Peur'.* Hurst and Blackett, London, 1889

CAMERON, J. *Our Tropical Possessions in Malayan India; being a descriptive account of Singapore, Penang, Province Wellesley, and Malacca; their peoples, products, commerce and government.* Smith & Elder, London, 1865

CHATFIELD, G. A. *The religions and festivals of Singapore.* D. Moore for Eastern Universities Press Ltd, Singapore, 1965

CHEW, H. L. *When Singapore was Syonan; being a brief account of what transpired during the three and a half years Japanese Occupation of Singapore.* Printed by G. H. Kiat, Singapore, 1945

CHIA, W. H. 'The Development of Painting in Singapore'. *Singapore Art Society. Souvenir Magazine,* 1969

CHIANG, T. C. *The Jurong Industrial Estate.* Institute of Southeast Asia, Nanyang University, Singapore, 1969

CHIN, K. O. *Malaya Upside Down.* Printed by Jitts & Co Ltd, 96 Robinson Road, Singapore, 1946

BIBLIOGRAPHY

CHONG, P. K., ed. *Problems in Political Development in Singapore.* McCutchan Pub Corp, California, 1968

COLLIS, M. *Raffles.* Faber & Faber, London, 1966

COMBER, L. *Chinese Ancestor Worship in Malaya.* Moore, Singapore, 1963

COMBER, L. *Chinese Temples in Singapore.* Eastern Universities Press Ltd, Singapore, 1958

COMBER, L. *An Introduction to Chinese Secret Societies in Malaya.* Moore, Singapore, 1957

COMBER, L. *The Traditional Mysteries of Chinese Secret Societies in Malaya.* Published by Moore for Eastern Universities Press Ltd, Singapore, 1961

CORNER, E. J. H. *Wayside Trees of Malaya.* Govt Print Off, Singapore, 1952

DAVIES, D. *Old Singapore.* D. Moore, Singapore, 1954.

Directory of Singapore Manufacturers. Singapore Manufacturers Association. Annual

DJAMOUR, J. *Malay Kinship and Marriage in Singapore.* Athlone Press, London, 1959

DJAMOUR, J. *The Muslim Matrimonial Court in Singapore.* University of London at the Athlone Press, London, 1966

DOGGETT, M. *Characters of Light: A Guide to the Buildings of Singapore.* D. Moore, Singapore, 1957

DRAKE, P. J. *Financial Development in Malaya and Singapore.* Australian National University Press, 1969

DRAKE, P. J. *Money and Banking in Malaya and Singapore.* Singapore, Malaysia Publications, Singapore, 1966

Economic Bulletin. Singapore International Chamber of Commerce. Monthly

EE, J. 'Chinese migration to Singapore, 1896–1941', *Journal of Southeast Asian History,* 2, 1961

FITZGERALD, C. P. *The Third China; the Chinese communities in Southeast Asia.* D. Moore, Books for the Australian Institute of International Affairs, Singapore, 1965

FOX, K. *Singapore; City of Contrasts.* Eastern Universities Press Ltd, Singapore, 1967

FREEDMAN, M. *Chinese Family and Marriage in Singapore.* HMSO, London, 1957

FREEDMAN, M. *The Chinese in South-east Asia; a longer view.* China Society, London, 1965

FUJII, T. *Singapore Assignment. Nippon Times,* Tokyo, 1943

BIBLIOGRAPHY

GAMBA, C. 'Chinese Associations in Singapore', *Royal Asiatic Society. Malaysian Branch. Journal*, 39 no 2, December 1966

GIBSON-HILL, C. A. 'The fishing boats operated from Singapore Islands', *Royal Asiatic Society. Malayan Branch. Journal*, 23 no 3, August 1950

GILMOUR, O. W. *With Freedom to Singapore*. Ernest Benn Ltd, London, 1950

GOH, K. S. *Some Problems of Industrialization*. Ministry of Culture, Singapore, 1963

Guide to Singapore Port Facilities, 1969. Guthrie Boustead Shipping Agencies, Singapore, 1969

Guide to the Employment Act 1968. Govt Print Off, Singapore, 1968

GUILLEMARD, L. *Trivial Fond Records*. Methuen, London, 1937

AL-HADI, S. A. *Malay Customs and Traditions*. Eastern Universities Press Ltd, Singapore, 1962

HALL, D. G. E. *A History of South-East Asia*, 3rd ed, Macmillan, London, 1968

HARRISON, J. L. *An Introduction to Mammals of Singapore and Malaya*. Malayan Nature Society, Singapore, 1966

Health in Singapore. Ministry of Health, Singapore, Annual

HENDERSON, M. R. *Common Malayan Wildflowers*. Longmans, London, 1961

HENDERSON, M. R. and ADDISON, G. H. *Malayan Orchid Hybrids*. Govt Print Off, Singapore, 1961

HUGHES, D. R. *The peoples of Malaya*. Published by D. Moore for Eastern Universities Press Ltd, Singapore, 1965

HUGHES, H. and YOU, P. S., ed, *Foreign Investment and Industrialization in Singapore*. Australian National University Press, 1969

150 Years of Education in Singapore. Publication Board TTC, Singapore, 1969.

JOHNSON, A. *Malayan Botany*. Eastern Universities Press Ltd, Singapore, 1965

JOHNSON, A. *A Student's Guide to the Ferns of Singapore Island*. University of Malaya Press, Singapore, 1960

JOHNSON, D. S. *An Introduction to the Natural History of Singapore*. Rayirath Publications, Kuala Lumpur, 1964

JOSEY, A. *Lee Kuan Yew*. D. Moore, Singapore, 1968

Journal of South East Asian History, 10 no 1 (Singapore Commemorative Issue. 150th Anniversary)

BIBLIOGRAPHY

KAHIN, G. T., ed. *Governments and Politics of South East Asia.* Cornell University Press, 1959

KAYE, B. *Upper Nankin Street, Singapore; a sociological study of Chinese households living in a densely populated area.* University of Malaya Press, Singapore, 1960

KIPLING, R. *From Sea to Sea.* Macmillan, London, 1900

LEASOR, J. *Singapore: The Battle that Changed the World.* Doubleday, Garden City NY, 1968

LEE KUAN YEW. *The Battle for Merger.* Govt Print Off, Singapore, 1962

LEE KUAN YEW. *The Essentials of Economic Growth.* Ministry of Culture, Singapore, 1969

LIM, C. S. and WONG, L, ed. *Management Development in Singapore.* Singapore Institute of Management, 1969

LIM, J. *Sold for Silver.* The World Publishing Co, London and New York, 1958

LOGAN, J. R., ed. *Journal of the Indian Archipelago and Eastern Asia 1847–62.* Printed at the Mission Press, Singapore, 1847–62

LOH, K. A. *Fifty Years of the Anglican Church in Singapore Island 1909–1959.* Dept of History, University of Singapore, Singapore, 1963

LU, S. *Face Painting in Chinese Opera.* MPH Publications, Singapore, 1968

McKIE, R. C. H. *This Was Singapore.* R. Hale, London, 1940

MA, R. and YOU, P. S. *The economy of Malaysia and Singapore.* Malaysia Publication. Singapore, 1966

MAKEPEACE, W., ed. *100 Years of Singapore.* 2 vols. J. Murray, London, 1921

MEDWAY, LORD. *The Wild Mammals of Malaya and Offshore Islands including Singapore.* Oxford University Press, London, 1969

MIALARET, J-P. *Hinduism in Singapore; a guide to the Hindu temples of Singapore.* Published for Asia Pacific Press by D. Moore, Singapore, 1969

MILLER, H. *Quiz on Malaysia and Singapore.* Pub by D. Moore for Asia Pacific Press, Singapore, 1970

MOORE, D. and J. *The First 150 Years of Singapore.* D. Moore in association with the Singapore International Chamber of Commerce, Singapore, 1969

MORRELL, R. G. R. *Common Malayan Butterflies.* Longmans, London, 1960

o   225

BIBLIOGRAPHY

NARASUMHAN, P. S. 'The Immigrant Communities of South East Asia', *Indian Quarterly*, January-March, 1947.

National Library Annual Report. Singapore.

NETTO, G. *Indians in Malaya: Historical facts and figures*. Pub by the author, Singapore, 1961

ONRAET, R. H. DE S. *Singapore—A Police Background*. D. Crisp, London, 1947

OOI, J. B. and CHIANG, H. D., ed. *Modern Singapore*. University of Singapore, 1969

OWEN, F. *The Fall of Singapore*. M. Joseph, London, 1960

PAPINEAU STUDIO. *Guide to Singapore and Spotlight on Malaysia*. Singapore, 1971

PARKINSON, C. N. *Britain In The Far East; The Singapore Naval Base*. D. Moore, Singapore, 1955

PAVITT, J. A. L. *First pharos of the eastern seas; Horsbrugh lighthouse*. D. Moore for Singapore Light Dues Board, Singapore, 1966

PEARSON, H. F. *A History of Singapore*. University of London Press, London, 1956

PEARSON, H. F. *People of Early Singapore*. University of London Press, 1955

PERCIVAL, A. E. *Operations of Malaya Command, from 8th December, 1941 to 15th February, 1942*. HMSO, London, 1948

PERCIVAL, A. E. *The War in Malaya*. Eyre & Spottiswoode, London, 1949

PORT OF SINGAPORE AUTHORITY. *Report and Accounts*, Singapore, Annual

PRIDMORE, F. *Coins and coinages of the Straits Settlements and British Malaya, 1786 to 1951*. Govt Print Off, Singapore, 1955. (Raffles Museum, Singapore. Memoirs, no 2)

PROBERT, H. A., compiler. *History of Changi*. Printed by Prison Industries in Changi Prison, Singapore, 1965

Public Housing in Singapore: a handbook of facts and figures. Ministry of Culture. Govt Print Off, Singapore, 1967

PURCELL, V. W. W. S. *The Chinese in Modern Malaya*, 2nd rev ed. Published by D. Moore for Eastern Universities Press Ltd, Singapore, 1960

PURCELL, V. W. W. S. *The Chinese in Southeast Asia*, 2nd ed. Oxford University Press, London, 1965

RAJARATNAM, S. *Asia's Unfinished Revolution and The World of Tomorrow*. 1966; *Challenge of confrontation*, 1964; *Malayan culture in the making,* 1960; *Malaysia and the World,* 1960–66; Ministry of Culture, Singapore, 1960–66

RAJA SINGAM, S. DURAI. *A Hundred Years of Ceylonese in Malaysia and Singapore (1867–1967).* Printed by N. T. Pillay, Kuala Lumpur, 1968

RAMACHANDRA, S. *Singapore Landmarks.* D. Moore for Eastern Universities Press Ltd, Singapore, 1961

ROFF, W. R. *The Origins of Malay Nationalism.* University of Malaya Press, Kuala Lumpur, 1967

SANDHU, K. S. *Indians in Malaya.* Cambridge University Press, London, 1969

SHERRY, N. *Conrad's Eastern World.* Cambridge University Press, London, 1966

Shipping Guide of Singapore. USAHA Advertising Corp, Singapore, 1969

SHORRICK, N. *Lion in the Sky.* Federal Publications, Kuala Lumpur, 1968

SIMON, I. *Singapore: Too Little, Too Late.* Published for Asia Pacific Press by D. Moore, Singapore, 1970

SINGAPORE. Chinese Chamber of Commerce. *Annual Report.* Singapore (in Chinese)

SINGAPORE. Chinese Chamber of Commerce. *List of Association and Firm Members of the Chinese Chamber of Commerce, Singapore.* Singapore. Irregular

SINGAPORE. Customs and Excise Dept. *Trade Classification and Customs Tariff.* Singapore, 1968

SINGAPORE. Department of Statistics. *Monthly Digest of Statistics.* Singapore

SINGAPORE. Dept of Statistics. *Report on the Census of Industrial Production.* Govt Print Off, Singapore. Irregular

SINGAPORE. Economic Development Board. *Annual Report.* Singapore

SINGAPORE. Economic Development Board. *The Jurong Story.* Singapore, 1967

SINGAPORE. Economic Development Division. Economics Section. *Singapore: State of the Economy.* Singapore. Bi-annual

Singapore External Trade Statistics. Govt Print Off, Singapore, Quarterly

Singapore Facts and Pictures. Ministry of Culture. Annual. Singapore

Singapore Guide and Street Directory. Govt Print Off, Singapore

227

BIBLIOGRAPHY

SINGAPORE. Indian Chamber of Commerce. *Annual Report.* Singapore

SINGAPORE. International Chamber of Commerce. *Annual Report.* Singapore

SINGAPORE. Laws, statutes, etc. *The good citizen's guide. Handbook of declarations, orders, rules and regulations, etc. issued by Gunseikan-bu (Military Administration Dept) Syonan Tokubetu-si (Municipality) and Johore Administration between February 2602 (1942) and March 2603 (1943).* Syonan-to, The Syonan Sinbun (English ed) 2603 (1943)

Singapore National Bibliography. National Library. Annual. Singapore

SINGAPORE. National Theatre Trust. *Annual Report.* Singapore

SINGAPORE. National Trades Union Congress. *The Problems of Workers in Developing countries; working papers presented by the Central Committee of the Singapore National Trades Union Congress, to the International Labour Seminar.* Singapore, 1965

SINGAPORE. Planning Dept. *Revised master plan.* Singapore, 1970

Social Services in Singapore. Ministry of Social Affairs. Annual. Singapore

Social Transformation in Singapore. Ministry of Culture. Govt Print Off. Singapore, 1964

Singapore Trade and Industry. Straits Times Press. Monthly, Singapore

Singapore Year Book: Govt Print Off, Singapore. Annual

Singapore Yearbook of Statistics. Govt Print Off, Singapore. Annual

SONG, O. S. *100 Years' History of the Chinese in Singapore.* University of Malaya Press. Singapore, 1967

STONE, H. *From Malacca to Malaysia,* 1400–1965. Harrap, London, 1966

Straits Times Annual. Straits Times Press, Singapore

Straits Times. Press cuttings from the *Straits Times : Riots in Singapore in July and Sept 1964,* compiled by References Dept, Library, University of Singapore. Singapore, 1964

Straits Times. Press cuttings from the *Straits Times : Trials,* compiled by Reference Dept, Library, University of Singapore. Singapore, 1967

TAE, Y. N. 'Singapore's One-Party System : Its Relationship to Democracy and Political Stability'. *Pacific Affairs,* 42 no 4. Winter 1969–70

TAN, H. B. *A Study of Commercial Banking Practices in Singapore.*

228

Economics Section. Economic Development Division. Singapore, 1969

TEIXEIRA, FR. M. *The Portuguese Missions in Malaya and Singapore 1511–1958.* Lisbon, 1963

THOMSON, G. G., ed. *Singapore's International Relations.* Lembaga Gerakan Pelajaran Dewasa. Singapore, 1966

TREGONNING, K. G. *Home Port Singapore: A History of the Straits Steamship Co Ltd, 1890–1965.* Oxford University Press, London, 1967

TREGONNING, K. G. *Malaysia and Singapore.* Rev ed. Pub by D. Moore Books for the Australian Institute of International Affairs, Singapore, 1966

TREGONNING, K. G. *Straits Tin; a brief account of the first seventy-five years of the Straits Trading Company, Limited, 1887–1962.* Straits Times Press, Singapore, 1962

TSUJI, M. *Singapore; The Japanese Version.* Translated by Margaret E. Lake. Edited by H. V. Howe. Sydney, Smith, 1960

TWEEDIE, M. W. F. *Common Malayan Birds.* Longmans, London, 1960

US BOARD ON GEOGRAPHIC NAMES. *Decision on names in the Federation of Malaya and Singapore.* Washington, 1952

WANG, GUNG-WU. *A Short History of the Nanyang Chinese.* Published by D. Moore for Eastern Universities Press Ltd, Singapore, 1959

WHEATLEY, P. *Impressions of the Malay Peninsula in Ancient Times.* Published by D. Moore for Eastern Universities Press Ltd, Singapore, 1964

WHEATLEY, P. *The Golden Khersonese.* University of Malaya Press, Kuala Lumpur, 1961

Who's Who: Malaysia and Singapore. Edited by J. Victor Morais. J. V. Morais, Kuala Lumpur, Annual.

WIJEYSINGHA, E. *A History of Raffles Institution, 1823–1963.* University Education Press, Singapore, 1963

WILLIAMS, L. E. *The Future of the Overseas Chinese in Southeast Asia.* Published for the Council on Foreign Relations by McGraw-Hill, New York, 1966

WILSON, D. *East Meets West Singapore.* Printed by Times Printers, Sdn Berhad, Singapore, 1970

WILSON, J. *The Singapore Rubber Market.* Eastern Universities Press Ltd, Singapore, 1958

WINSLEY, T. M. *A History of the Singapore Volunteer Corps,*

BIBLIOGRAPHY

1854–1937; being also a historical outline of volunteering in Malaya. With a foreword by Sir Thomas Shenton Whitelegge Thomas and an introduction by W. G. S. Dobbie. Govt Print Off, Singapore, 1938

WINSTEDT, R. *The Malays: A Cultural History.* Routledge and Kegan Paul, London, 1961

WURTZBURG, C. E. *Raffles of the Eastern Isles.* Edited by Clifford Witting. Hodder & Stoughton, London, 1954

YEH, S. H. K. and LEE, Y. S. *Housing Conditions in Singapore.* Economic Research Centre, University of Singapore, Singapore, 1968

YEO, R. 'Poetry in English in Singapore and Malaysia'. *Singapore Book World* 1 no 1, April 1970, Singapore

YONG, C. F. 'A Preliminary Study of Chinese Leadership in Singapore, 1900–1941', *Journal of Southeast Asian History*, 9 no 2, September 1968

FICTION

CLAVELL, J. *King Rat.* M. Joseph, London, 1963

CONRAD, J. *Lord Jim.* J. M. Dent, London, 1900

GLASKIN, G. M. *A Lion in the Sun.* Barrie & Rockcliff, London, 1960

KAYE, T. *David, from Where He Was Lying.* Cape, London, 1962

MAUGHAM, W. S. *The Complete Short Stories,* vol. 3. Heinemann, London, 1966

MOORE, D. *The Sacrifice and Other Stories.* A. Barker, London, 1957

SHERRY, S. *Street of the Small Night Market.* Cape, London, 1966

THOMAS, L. *The Virgin Soldiers.* Constable, London, 1966

ACKNOWLEDGEMENTS

In my search for information about Singapore, I have been helped with great courtesy and patience by many people, both Singaporeans and expatriates, and I wish to thank in particular Miss G. Chung, Professor Nan Elliott, Shiri Mulgaokar, Pang Cheng Lian, Mrs P. H. Poh, Miss R. Quah, Mr S. T. Ratnam and Mrs Lily Tan.

Dr D. S. Johnson and Dick Wilson were kind enough to read and criticise parts of my manuscript, and Mrs Hedwig Anuar, Mr B. Nair and Mr K. R. S. Vas were all generous with their time and knowledge in assisting me to obtain illustrations for the book : I am most grateful for the trouble they took. Finally I should like to thank Juminah binte Kamis, a very patient typist.

INDEX

233

235

INDEX

INDEX